pottery

A complete introduction to the craft of pottery

Jolyon Hofsted

Designed by and produced under the supervision of

William and Shirley Sayles

PAN BOOKS LTD: LONDON AND SYDNEY

FOREWORD

The craft of pottery, growing as it has on both avocational and professional levels since the end of World War II, has developed a myriad of new facets. One of these is the reflection in many potters' efforts of the current expressions in painting and sculpture. This is true of the work of Jolyon Hofsted, the author of this book and one of the United States' outstanding young craftsmen. The pots which come from his studio have broken the moulds of convention to become fresh, spontaneous expressions of the exciting age in which we live. This same spirit, also contained in the content of this book, imbues his classes in ceramics at The Brooklyn Museum Art School, Queens College, and such summer institutions as Haystack Mountain School of Crafts. The beginner in the field of pottery could not be in better hands. The chapters that follow give you not only the fundamentals of ceramic techniques, practical advice on tools and equipment, and a prodigious number of full-colour illustrations, but a series of imaginative projects which can be done at home with a minimum of equipment – and which allow room for and encourage individual experimentation. The craft of pottery is one of the most challenging of all the hand arts, and under the guidance of Jolyon Hofsted you are off to a most auspicious start.

Hal Halverstadt
Managing Editor, CRAFT HORIZONS

First British edition published 1972 by Pan Books Ltd,
Cavaye Place, London SW10 9PG
ISBN 0 330 23407 2

2nd Printing 1974

Copyright © 1967 by Western Publishing Company, Inc

Printed by Cripplegate Printing Co Ltd , London and Edenbridge

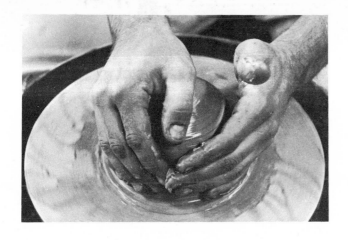

Contents

Acknowledgement

*In the course of preparing this book many craftsmen
were asked for photographic examples of their work,
and their cooperation was very gratifying – thanks
go to them and to the Brooklyn Museum of Art and to
the American Craftsmen's Council for lending photographic material from their collections.*
*Special thanks are also due to those who have assisted
in the preparation of this book:*

Hal Halverstadt, *Consultant*
Betty MacDonald, *Design*
Louis Mervar and James Dura, *Photography*
Robert Beame, *Artist*
Olivia Buehl, *Picture Research*

Introduction

The growing interest in handcrafts – not just pottery but all the hand arts – is the result of our need for the individual element, the human touch, in this age of mass production and standardization. Although the composition may be finer, the same clay used by potters to make unique bowls, vases, wall panels, and ceramic sculptures is used in the construction of skyscrapers on the rise in major cities as well as the drainage tile, plumbing fixtures, and electric insulators that make up the vascular systems of these structures. But this is part of the fascination of clay: that this inexpensive material, dug from the earth and refined, then mixed with water, can with a complex of equipment be moulded into the shapes of industry and with an absolute minimum of tools be made into objects of aesthetic distinction that often take their places with the art achievements of history.

Clay is one of the oldest of all craft mediums and dates back to prehistoric cultures. Originally forms were built up free-hand or on a simple mould and dried in the sun. A variety of outer coatings were added to minimize porosity. With the discovery of fire, it was found that by placing clay vessels on a bed of coals they became much less fragile and, in turn, able to withstand heat. The potter's wheel to form objects and the kiln for firing were subsequent technical improvements, and, with the exception of the refinement of these and the research in glaze development, the methods of pottery making have not changed over six thousand years.

Style, on the other hand, has been the variable factor. The early ware made by the potters of East and West were vessels of coarse, impure, roughly textured clay sometimes with painted decoration. As glaze was invented, the decorative possibilities of ceramics expanded. The

Right: Greek Attic black figure amphora, about 530 BC. Incised decoration with touches of red and white 'paint'. The Eugene Schaefer Collection. Courtesy of the Newark Museum

Early Egyptian vase illustrates the enduring character of pottery. Detail of wall painting depicting vase being made. Tomb of Rekhmara, about 1475 BC. Courtesy of the Brooklyn Museum and the Bettmann Archive

Bottle with slip decoration, unglazed, from Nazca, Peru. Courtesy of the Brooklyn Museum

Chinese Neolithic vase with slip decoration, un-glazed. Courtesy of the Brooklyn Museum

American Indian jug, with slip decoration, un-glazed, from Chaco, New Mexico AD 900–1400

medium reached a pinnacle in the ancient world with the vases produced in Athens and the surrounding region, called Attica. These ceramic masterpieces were the product of inspired collaboration between potter and painter; the latter creating in glaze the dynamic figure drawings which have remained a powerful influence on Western art from before the Age of Pericles to Picasso. At the opposite end of the spectrum in the history of European ceramics were the elaborately modelled porcelain figures of the eighteenth century. These were created by both European and Oriental potters for display in European palaces. Although Eastern potters continued to produce work of distinction, ceramics became as overblown as the societies that produced it.

With the industrial revolution, production-line pottery was greatly increased. The ware turned out was profusely decorated with transfer-printed scenes of sailing ships and flora and fauna, all with limited or no aesthetic value. Artists were the first to react to this treatment of a once noble craft and began dabbling in the medium themselves, first in designing and decorating, but then in actual potting. By the time arts and crafts societies were organized in the 1880s, pottery was a popular craft for artists, who quite naturally looked to the Orient. After the First World War, however, interested craftsmen attending the pioneering Bauhaus school of design opened in Berlin sought out a local folk potter who taught them ceramics in a revolutionary way. He and his students began producing traditional, functional wares in simple techniques that were not unlike the earliest recorded pottery, and, in their reassessment of the direction ceramics was taking, were in great part responsible for restoring the medium to one of distinction.

Polychrome Delft plate, Dutch c. 1700. Typical of the period when decoration dominated form. Courtesy of the Brooklyn Museum

In many countries, the aesthetic of primitive and folk pottery is the closest of all types of contemporary taste. Using techniques that reflect their knowledge and understanding of the history of pottery, modern ceramists have tended to use clay bodies which offer the most interesting textures, often finding these decoration in themselves, without the need of glaze or other treatments. With the exception of a stream of the avant-garde ceramists who have revived the use of metallic lustre glazes and other materials to create eye-stopping Pop art in clay, the trend is away from decoration for decoration's sake to an exploration and revelation of the basic qualities of clay and glaze.

Another interesting direction in modern ceramics is towards the unique, one-of-a-kind object. Although there are still many outstanding potters who are involved in production ware, it is becoming more and more apparent that handmade pottery for utilitarian use is an anachronism. Mass production and the new materials of industry have been able to give the consumer a range of handsome functional ware at such economical prices that the potter today cannot afford to compete in this area. Although possibly against his will, he has been freed from producing repetitive pieces and can today take his craft in any one of a thousand directions. And the range of work he is producing is truly great: from handsome, sturdy one-of-a-kind casseroles and storage jars, to monumental murals in clay, to the most abstract sculptural forms.

As a beginner, from the instructions in this book you will be able to make a variety of projects. Basic terminology of the medium, the hand-building techniques, and the wheel method are given. This experience with ceramics will teach a knowledge of clay and open up some of its possibilities. Clay affords the amateur and professional alike a way of expressing themselves with their hands – and with an inexpensive material.

Typical salt-glazed stoneware crock, by Edmands & Co, Massachusetts, c. 1850–1868

Earthenware Victorian pitcher with all-over relief pattern. By E. & W. Bennett, Baltimore, 1832. Courtesy of the Brooklyn Museum

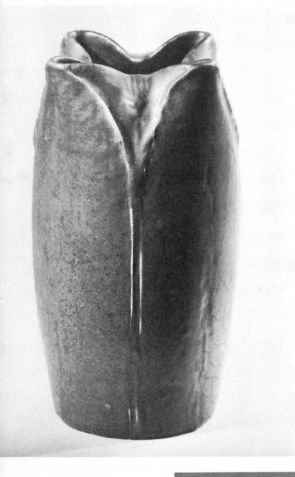

Earthenware 'Art Nouveau' vase in 'cucumber green', 203 mm (8 in.) high. Made by the Grueby Faience Co, Boston, 1897. Courtesy of the Brooklyn Museum

Contemporary wheel-thrown bottles and plate with simple brush decoration by Toshiko Takaezu. Photo by Barney Burstein

Hand-built slab and coil teapots of unusual design, by James Leedy, illustrate the contrast between the work of today's craftsmen and that of mass-produced wares

Slab built pot by Beverly Aldrich

Large coil bottle, unfired, by the author

The Slab

A slab of clay is exactly what the term implies, a ball or hunk of clay rolled out to an even thickness with a large dowel or rolling pin, and the rough edges trimmed off. Much of the contemporary pottery that you see in shops and exhibitions is, in fact, made from slabs joined together, and this forming technique, along with coil-building, is the basis of the projects in this book. In working with the slab (pages 34–47), you will find that it lends itself not only to geometric shapes but also to more spontaneous ones, such as the vase above. This pot was made of six slabs – two for the bottom half, two for the upper section, and two for the handles.

The Coil

The technique of coiling goes back in time as far as pottery itself and is the process which eventually led to the wheel method. With the hands, clay is rolled into long coils which are joined and circled round and round to build a vessel or other form. In the top photograph, I have worked the coils one quarter of the way up of what will be a large coil jar about 915 mm (3 ft) high. This pot was formed in little less than an hour. The beginning potter could work just as quickly, but with this exception the coil projects in this book (pages 49–55) are more modest in scale, since the work you make will have to be fired in the kiln size available.

Small vase by R. L. Rosenbaum

Wheel-thrown casserole by Karen Karnes

Combining Slab and Coil

Since the two major approaches to hand-built pottery are slab and coil, I would like to point out how well these methods can be combined. A good example is the pot above made from the slabs and coils in the photograph at the top of the page. (In the upper photograph left-hand corner is a hand-carved plaster stamp, used to decorate the pot.) The body is slab-built, and the decoration pieces of coil and stamping. Later when you learn how to throw on the wheel, you can add a wheel-thrown spout to a slab bottle, slab handles to a thrown vase, etc. The variations are limitless (Combined Methods projects pages 65–73).

Wheel Throwing

To watch an experienced potter throw a ball of clay onto the spinning potter's wheel and then to see him manipulate and control the plastic material so that it literally grows into a full-blown form is an exciting and sometimes awe-inspiring experience. As you become more involved with the craft of pottery you will eventually want to learn wheel throwing yourself. One of the advantages of this method is that forms can be shaped rapidly and, with practice, they can be easily duplicated. The step-by-step demonstration on pages 80–82 will help to acquaint you with the basic procedures of this exacting process.

Press mould trivet by the author

Plate made in the slip cast method

The Press Mould

There are several ways of making pottery in moulds in order to repeat shapes, such as bowls or mugs, or flat shapes with rich surface decoration such as tiles of the hot plate shown above. One of the most direct is the press mould method in which a slab of clay is laid over a plaster mould and pressed onto it (pages 56–7). The excess clay is then trimmed away, the surface smoothed, and the clay form removed. The mould to make the hot plate, shown above, was made from a slab of hardened plaster with the shape carved out. A moulded form though repeated many times can still retain a fresh and individual look by applying additions such as handles or pedestals, textures or glazes.

Slip Casting

In factory production, slip casting moulds are used to make objects such as dinner plates in exact duplicate – with the decoration also standardized. However, this process is also used by the hand potter as a short cut to sturdy plates or platters which can then be finished individually (pages 58–9), usually with painted glazes. A slip casting mould, which can be purchased, consists of two halves, made of plaster, with a cavity in between. Slip, which is liquid clay, is poured into the space inside. After the slip has hardened, the plate is removed from the mould. Slips are available from any ceramic supply house and come in a wide range of colours.

Plant holder made in the sand cast method

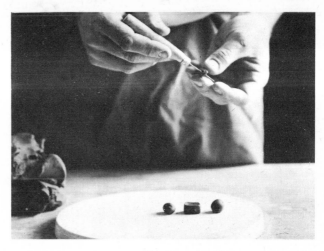

Necklace by Frances Schneider

Sand Casting

Sand casting, another popular mould technique (see pages 62–3), allows you to make large, strongly textured pieces, such as the garden bottle above, and to repeat what you have made. For this or other container shapes, a model for *half* of the form is built up in wet sand and the surface textured with a blunt stick or other tool. Layers of plaster are poured over the sand mould and allowed to harden. A slab of clay is laid over the inside of the shell and pressed into it. After the clay has stiffened enough to hold its shape, it is removed, and the process repeated. To make the plant holder, the two halves that are made are joined by scoring them, adding slip and pressing them together.

Egyptian Paste

Egyptian paste is a kind of clay that duplicates closely the material from which the ancients made their ceramic beads. Jewellery can also be made with regular clay, but this must be dried, then bisque-fired, glazed, strung on nichrome wire, and fired again. Egyptian paste needs only to be shaped and fired. There are two recipes on page 74, one giving you a dry, matte surface, the other a glossy surface. The materials can be purchased from any pottery supplier. Egyptian paste can be handled in the same fashion as regular clay: it can be rolled, made into slabs, patted, pinched, or any of the other various forming methods from which beads can be cut or otherwise made.

(Top left) Texture achieved by uniform pinching. Stoneware covered jar, 229 mm (9 in.) high, by Marlis Schratter

(Top right) All-over carved design supplies textural interest. Vase by C. H. Brown. Photo by Judith Gefter

(Right) Unglazed rough-textured clay produces its own texture. By Robert Winokur

(Bottom) Example of slab construction lending textural excitement. Bottle by Louis B. Raynor. Courtesy of the Smithsonian Institute, Washington, D.C.

Texture

When the basic form of a pot has been made either with slabs, coils, on the wheel, in a mould, by casting, or with a combination of these, there are two ways of decorating or finishing it. The surface of the clay can be textured, or the entire pot, or parts of it, can be glazed. Texturing is a blanket term for the processes that give variation to the clay surface; some of the methods used are carving, scratching, stamping, adding coils, slabs, or bits of clay. Tools can be any that do the proper job, from a professional sgraffito tool to pencils, nails, or your hands. Even such basic means as pinching can be effective on certain forms. As you can see in the illustrations here, texture can enhance a shape, or it can dominate it.

(Top right) Rough-textured stoneware with white slip and a carved motif. By Sophia and John Fenton. Photo by Brigadier Studios

(Bottom left) Hand-built vase with rough-textured clay and brushed decoration. By Sophia and John Fenton

(Bottom centre) An example of decoration built up with additional clay. Vase by Gertrud Englander

(Bottom right) Partially glazed bottle with stamp impressed decoration. By Robert Winokur

Clays

Clay, the basic raw material of pottery, is plentiful and inexpensive. There are clay beds in many parts of the country where clay is mined not so much for pottery as for industrial uses. Most clay, as it comes from the ground, is full of impurities and is mixed with rocks, pebbles, and sand. It must, therefore, be refined before it can be used by industry or the potter. Many craftsmen enjoy digging their own clay and processing it, but since this is such a time-consuming operation, and good, reasonably-priced clay bodies are available almost everywhere, we will concentrate on their use rather than on how to prepare them.

What is clay? Essentially, it is granite-type rock that has decomposed into tiny particles over millions of years. It is found in the same position as the parent rock – these are known as primary clays – or in the bottoms of lakes and lagoons, the particles having been washed there from the high rock formations – these are known as secondary clays. The plasticity or workability of clay is of primary importance to the potter, and the fineness of the individual clay particle has much to do with its plasticity. Since the original particle size of the secondary clays was small enough to have been carried by water, these are finer, and

(Left) Stoneware teapot, wheel-thrown and partially glazed. By Karen Karnes. Photo by Henry Ries

(Right) Earthenware vases, the one in rear with sgraffito decorations, by Nancy Boyd. Photo by Hans van Nes

therefore more plastic, than the residual type. It is the secondary ones which make up the bodies that you will use.

Before we list the various secondary clays, let us take a look at one of the most important steps in the craft of pottery – the firing process. After you have finished making a pot, the next step is to let it dry completely, so that all moisture is gone from the clay. The pot is then placed in a kiln or furnace which is heated to temperatures ranging from 650°C to 1300°C, depending on the type of clay body from which the pot was made. This is called firing, and the object here is to heat the elements which comprise the clay to the point where they fuse. The colour of clay is also transformed during this process and what you had

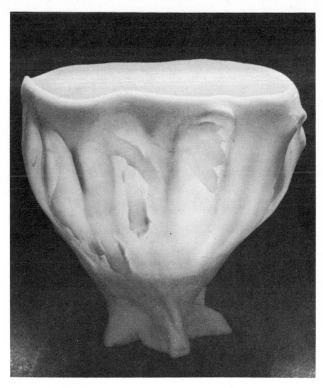

High-fired porcelain bowl, unglazed, 254 mm (10 in.) high, by Rudolf Staffel. Courtesy of Craft Horizons

known in the workshop as a dull grey becomes a warm and appealing off-white buff, tan or dark red. Fired clay always has a matt surface; the glossy surface that you have seen on pottery is called glaze, and this will be discussed shortly.

First among the secondary clays are the following: kaolins, ball clays, fireclays, stoneware clays, and earthenware clays. Most generally used by potters today are stoneware clays which generally fire to a light grey colour and mature between 1250°C and 1300°C. These result in ware that is hard and vitreous, ideal for pots that must be handled a great deal or withstand heat, such as cooking ware.

Kaolin sedimentary kaolin is a natural clay composed mainly of silica and alumina and when formed makes the finest whiteware body available. It withstands a very high degree of heat.

Ball clay resembles kaolin in chemical content, but is finer and more plastic. When fired, it is almost white.

Fireclay resembles kaolin in chemical content, but contains more iron causing the clay to turn buff-coloured when fired. Its endurance of high heat enables it to be used as firebrick and as lining and shelves for the kiln.

Stoneware is usually made from several natural clays plus alumina and silica, to give it the desirable characteristics of plasticity, colour, and the correct firing temperature. When fired, it becomes hard and vitreous, able to hold water without being glazed. It generally fires to a light grey but sometimes may be tan or even slightly reddish.

Earthenware is usually made from a natural clay and is low fired, as opposed to stoneware which is high fired, maturing at a kiln temperature between 950°C and 1150°C. The body is non-vitreous and will not hold a liquid unless glazed. The colour after firing is usually buff or red.

Porcelain is made from a prepared body containing kaolin, ball clay, feldspar, and flint. Hard, non-absorbent, of pristine whiteness, translucent in thin areas, it requires the highest fire of all pottery wares – up to 1450°C. Since it is not very pliable and requires more skill to work, it is not recommended as a clay body for beginning craftsmen.

The Firing Process

Since the compounds which make up clay and glaze undergo many chemical changes during the firing cycle, this is a process that takes a certain amount of care. In this area, there is no substitute for actual experience. Depending upon the temperatures to which your kiln must be heated and *slowly* cooled, the firing cycle can take up to ten or even twelve hours. Firing to low earthenware temperatures should take eight hours, and never less than six. Pointers on firing a kiln are on pages 86 and 87.

Oxidation firing is the normal firing in all types of kilns. The kiln you use will be heated either by electricity, gas, or oil. An electric kiln *always* has an oxidizing fire since there is no combustible fuel to consume the oxygen, which is always present. The results of oxidation are generally predictable, and you can obtain a wide range of bright and glossy colours with oxidation glazes. The common temperatures for oxidizing fire are under 1200°C.

Reduction firing is done during certain periods of the firing cycle in gas or oil kilns to develop the particular colour characteristics of reduction glazes. After beginning with oxidizing fire, the burners and air intake are so regulated as to get incomplete combustion, which releases carbon into the kiln. This is known as reducing the atmosphere. Since carbon has a great affinity for oxygen, it will, in this atmosphere, steal it from the iron and copper oxides which are part of reduction glazes. When either of these are deprived of their oxygen, they remain suspended in glaze as pure colloidal metal. The normally green copper glaze then becomes a luscious ruby red, occasionally flecked with blues and purples, while iron oxide loses its usual brownish-red colour and takes on a variety of quiet grey-green tones. Reduction firing is best done at high temperatures – between 1200°C and 1300°C. Although the range of colours available with reduction glazes is small, they more than make up for this with their subtlety and quiet beauty.

(Right) Subtle decoration achieved by salt beading built up on ridged surfaces. Salt-glazed pitcher by A. C. Garzio

(Below) Reduction firing produced this rich, glossy glaze. Bowl by Lillian Samenfeld

Salt glazing is a unique process in which raw clay pots are placed in a kiln and common table salt thrown in when the body is mature. At the completion of firing the pots are covered with a variegated brown and grey glaze. What happens here is that the salt combines with the silica in the body, usually stoneware, to form a handsome and particularly durable glaze. The process was discovered by German potters in the fifteenth century when they threw salt into the fire box of their wood-burning kilns. Salt glazing can be done today in down-draft open-fire kilns by throwing salt in through the opening around the burner or through special ports in the sides. Once a kiln is used for salt glazing, however, it is difficult to fire other kinds of ware in it with certainty; the interior of the kiln becomes coated with the glaze which is somewhat volatile. As your interest in the medium develops, you may come across a salt glazing kiln or decide to experiment with the technique in a workshop situation. The results will be well worth while. A point to remember: the interiors of salt-glazed pots have to be treated in the traditional fashion, that is, glazed before firing, as the salt vapours will not reach them.

CAUTION: A by-product of toxic chlorine gas is given off during the firing. Always be sure to fire in a well-ventilated area.

Raku is a process developed by Japanese potters and used by them for making tea ceremonial ware. The results are invariably distinctive. A pot made from a porous clay body is treated with low-fire lead glazes and placed in a kiln 800°C to 950°C, in a bisque state. When the glazes are smooth and shiny, the pot is removed with tongs and dropped into a bed of smoke-producing materials – wood chips, leaves, or straw. The smoke from these darkens any unglazed clay and causes local reduction in the glazed areas. After ten to fifteen minutes, the pot is plunged into cold water, and the process is complete. Instructions are found on page 90.

Oxidation firing of stoneware biscuit jar created this iron-spotted effect. By Robert Turner

Milky glaze is a typical result of Raku firing technique. By the author

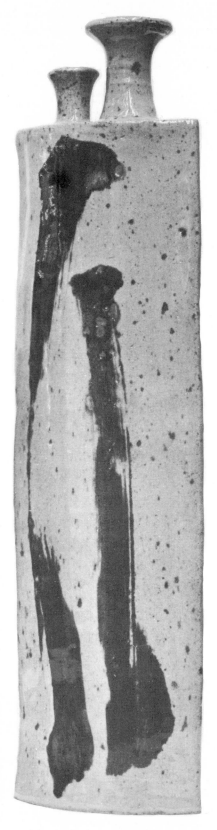

(Top) Wax resist with mat glaze slip decoration. Container with cover by Ralph Baccera. Photo by Sam Calder

(Right) Colouring oxide adds strong design element to vase by Vivika and Otto Heino

(Bottom left) White glaze slip with brushed decoration. Stoneware tea caddy by John Glick. Photo by Betty S. Wagner

(Bottom centre) Crackle glazed bottle by C. H. Brown. Photo Judith Gefter

Glaze

Glaze produces a layer of glass crystals on the clay surface. Its purpose is both decorative and, since it waterproofs a vessel, useful. Glaze is applied in a liquid state, and when the pot is fired it reacts and melts forming a thin layer of glass. There are low-fire glazes, those which melt at 850°C to 1100°C, and high-fire glazes, those which need temperatures of 1150°C to 1300°C (see page 92). Within these categories there are also many types: crackle, matt, crystalline, slip, lustre, reduction, and salt glazes. The common procedure for glazing is first to bisque fire a pot – that is, fire it to a temperature of about 950°C. A raw, dry clay vessel is fragile, and a bisque firing makes it hard enough to be handled safely yet porous enough to absorb glaze readily. For a beginner prepared glazes are recommended, but remember that specific glazes are designed for certain clays and kiln temperatures.

(Top right) Porcelain glazed bowl, 380 mm (15 in.) diameter, by Ann Stockton. Photo by Ferdinand Boesch

(Bottom left) Beaten porcelain bottle with crystalline glaze. By Herbert Sanders

(Bottom right) Slip trailing technique used to decorate bottle, by Tom McMillin. Courtesy of Craft Horizons

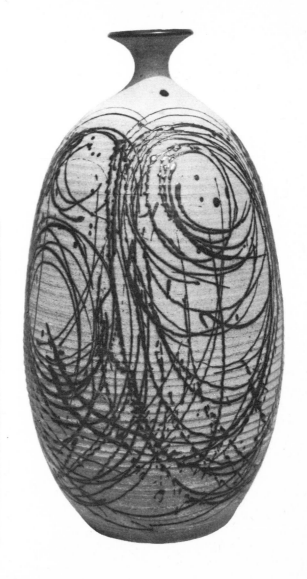

The Workshop

Although most beginning potters start with an absolute minimum of equipment – and this is certainly recommended – a growing interest in the medium will necessitate buying or making various items. The plan below, of an ideal studio for a professional potter, will help you plan ahead for the best use of available space. The important thing to keep in mind is the relationship of the setup to your own work procedure, such as the damp box and raw materials near the forming area or the kiln in a far corner of the studio. If you are handy with a saw, hammer, and nails, most of the plan below can be built rather than purchased.

1	Bench work and storage	**9**	Damp box
2	Spray booth	**10**	Sink
3	Glaze and chemical storage	**11**	Wedging board
4	Storage – Cabinets and shelves	**12**	Potter's wheel
5	Kiln supplies	**13**	Tool storage
6	Kiln	**14**	Finishing tables
7	Desk	**15**	Plaster table
8	Raw materials	**16**	Display cabinet

Floor plan of a workshop showing a logical work arrangement. Note that any arrangement to be convenient and efficient should apply to your work procedure

(Below) a sufficient number of shelves are necessary to store tools and materials, ware that is drying and waiting to be fired, and completed pieces

Materials and Equipment

Basically the only items necessary for making pots with slabs and coils, aside from the kiln for firing, are clay and your hands, but there are a few tools which will be valuable. These are inexpensive and can be obtained from ceramics supply dealers or else improvised. Shown here, they are:

Ruler – Used for measuring or as a beater for shaping work.

Chinese brush – Ideal for applying glaze. Small paint brushes of various sizes can also be used.

Wire trimming tool – For shaping and carving pots.

Pin (mounted on a handle) – Can be purchased, but a hat pin stuck through a cork will work as well.

Pencil – A tool for which you will find many uses.

Wire – For cutting through clay while wedging and slicing slabs (pages 26–7). Attach a 610 mm length to handles of some type – wood sticks, buttons, anything you can hold onto.

'Fettling' or potters knife – Best purchased, but a table knife or painter's palette knife will do.

As to the clay you will use, different types fire at different temperatures, so it would be ideal to know in advance what kind of kiln will be available to you. If you don't know the kind of kiln you will be using, the best solution is to choose a clay with a wide firing range, one that can be used successfully at different temperatures. Look for one which will fire from 1038°C to 1177°C.

Although most professional potters make their own glazes, I recommend that readers of this book buy prepared ones. These are again determined by your clay and the firing range of the kiln you are using.

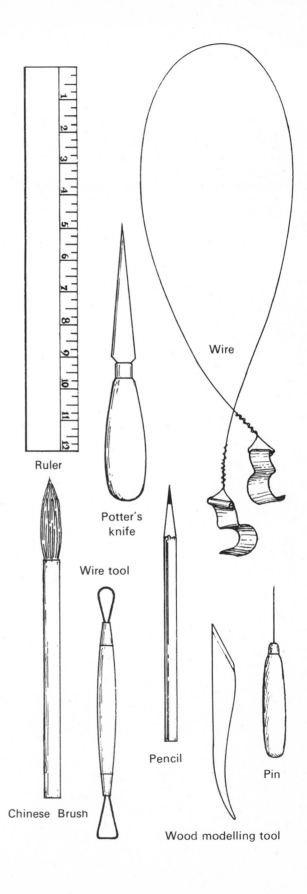

Ruler

Potter's knife

Wire

Wire tool

Pencil

Pin

Chinese Brush

Wood modelling tool

Cutting the clay with the wire

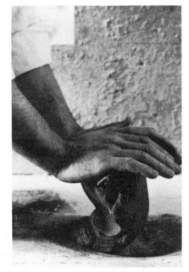

The kneading process

Checking for air bubbles

Wedging

There are two approaches to wedging which will give you clay of a smooth even texture, and I suggest that you try both to see which is most suitable for you.

The first approach is often called the 'cut and slam' method. Take the lump of clay you are planning to work with and cut it in half, either by pushing it against a wedging wire stretched across your table-top or by holding a wire taut in your hands and pushing it through the clay. Throw one half down hard on the table; then throw the other half on top of the first. Cut and slam again and continue this procedure until all the air has been driven out of the clay. Your clay is 'ready' when you can cut through it with a wire at any point and find it completely smooth.

The second approach is called 'kneading'. The clay is cut and thrown as above but then worked and pressed with your hands until smooth, much like working bread dough.

Overall, you will save time and energy by wedging a large amount of clay before you begin to work, so that you will not have to repeat the process for each pot. Store what you don't use immediately in a damp box (page 24) or wrap in polythene. Once clay is wedged, it stays wedged, so there is no danger of doing work which will have to be repeated.

You will now want to try your hand at making slabs and coils for the projects that follow. The only other basic process used in this book is making a rounded ball of clay for the 'pinch' pot project on page 32. This is done simply by rolling a hunk of clay between your hands until it is fairly symmetrical.

Making Slabs

There are two ways of making slabs. In one, two guide sticks are placed, on a piece of hessian, as far apart as the slab is to be wide. The thickness of the sticks will determine the thickness of the slab, and I would suggest using sticks 15 mm ($\frac{1}{2}$ in.) thick. Put a large ball of clay on the hessian between the sticks and roll it out with a rolling pin or dowel, resting whichever you use on the two pieces of wood. This will give you slabs of an even thickness. Peel the clay off the hessian and trim the ragged edges. Although hessian is used so that clay won't stick to the table, it also gives one side of the slab an interesting texture. You might keep this in mind for later use.

The other method of making slabs is to take a big hunk of prepared clay and, on a table or a flat surface, pound it into a rectangle the size of a shoe box. Slabs can then be sliced off the squared piece of clay with a wire. Although this approach will not give you completely even slabs, it is much faster and is the method I prefer.

Either way, always give the slabs a chance to stiffen before using them.

Making Coils

There are also two ways of making coils. For small, even ones roll out balls of clay on a freshly dampened table, so that the clay remains moist and does not break. Larger coils can be made by squeezing. Both methods are shown below.

Shaping clay ball for pinch project

Rolling out small uniform coils

Forming large uniform coils by squeezing

Making slabs by rolling out clay

Cutting slabs from clay block

Experimenting With Texture

Before beginning to build clay forms of any kind, introduce yourself to the material in order to discover its possibilities as well as its limitations. The best way to go about this is to take a hunk of prepared clay in your hands and play with it. Squeeze it, bend it, pound it, pinch it. Fold or bend various thicknesses of it. Find out how far you can extend its plastic possibilities. For instance, does clay crack when you bend it? The more you handle your material in an exploratory way, the sooner answers to questions such as this will be second nature.

When you have spent some time in this meeting process take a big lump of clay and make it into a flat slab by pounding and slapping on a table or on the floor. You now have a surface on which to investigate what kinds of texture different objects

will make. Elementary as it may sound, when clay is in its plastic state, *anything* pressed on it can vary the surface. Take a look at the examples of textures on pages 16–17 as well as those on the opposite page and then use whatever comes to mind on the slab you have made: the prongs of a fork, the end of it, a spoon, bolts, a coin, a pencil, a knife blade. If you have access to professional pottery tools, find out what these will do. Then remember that with your hands you can dig into clay, hit it, scratch it, brush it, gouge it. As stated above, anything and everything makes texture, but certain objects and methods produce more surface excitement than others.

Another method of patterning a slab of clay, one that will be used from time to time in the projects that follow, is to add coils or other pieces of clay to a surface, then beat them in with a stick. The effect is subtle and intriguing.

Almost any object can be used to impart texture to clay, and one tool can be used in different ways. Here a beater makes ridges by digging and patting

Dabbing with a brush, dotting with a finger nail, or making depressions with a sharp or blunt tool end are some examples of how to texture clay

Textural decoration in sgraffito technique achieved by scratching out a design through a layer of applied slip. Bottle by Richard Peeler

Pattern made by applying small coils to rough surface

Making Plaster Stamps

Besides using 'found objects', conventional pottery tools, and your hands to texture the surface of your work, simple stamps of your own design can be used to pattern the clay while still damp. This is a decorative device which dates back to pre-Christian times and probably began as a way of signing pots. Many potters today, in fact, use stamps in the form of a seal or signature to identify their work.

Stamps can be used singly or in combination, and there are a number of ways to make them. One of the more common is to carve a stamp out of wet clay. When fired, and therefore rock hard, it can be used to imprint fresh clay. Detail can be achieved in stamps carved out of plaster, however, and this is the method of stamp making described here.

The first step is to make small blocks of plaster. You can buy plaster in powdered form at any hardware or building supply store, but be sure to specify plaster of Paris or casting plaster. Sifting gently to prevent lumps, add one cup dry plaster to one cup of water. If possible, mix them in an old can which can be discarded when you are finished. When the mixture is lump free, pour it into small paper cups and let harden.

Two points to remember: be sure to add plaster to water, not water to plaster, and don't pour any of the mixture down a sink drain. It will harden and clog the pipes.

Pour plaster into paper cup

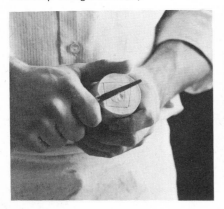

Tear cup from hardened plaster

Incise design in plaster

Develop design of stamp

Refine design

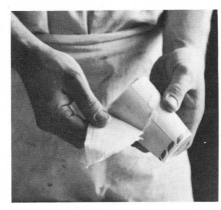

Finished stamp and test impression

When the plaster is solid, tear the paper off. You now have several blocks of uniform size. Sketch a variety of simple designs on them with a pin or pencil, then carve the plaster with a knife or an old umbrella spoke. Small wood-carving tools also work well if you happen to have some. Plaster becomes harder the longer it sets, so it is a good idea to do the rough or major carving when it has just reached a solid state. Cleaning and sharpening of lines are best done after a few hours. As you are carving, stop from time to time and press the stamp into a piece of flat clay, so that you can see how the design is coming.

Stamped decoration used on bottles, 127 mm (5 in.) high, by Paula Winokur. Photo by Robert Winokur

The variety of plaster stamp designs range from fine detailed patterns for making delicate impressions, to bolder shapes to give more massive decoration on the clay

An interesting tile can develop by a variety of stamps being impressed in the clay, as shown below

The Pinch Pot

The pinch method is about the simplest way to make a pot. Since these pots are usually small and do not require tools in the actual forming, they offer to the beginner the best way of acquiring a feeling for the clay. Take advantage of this 'getting acquainted' period before going to work on the slab and coil projects.

The idea is basic: a ball of wedged clay is pressed or pinched into a small shape. For this version, texturing is added at the end to make a small-scale vase. There are a number of ways you can use such pots, as containers for dried flowers or small fresh ones, as cigarette holders, or as holders for paper clips and pins. I suggest that you follow the process through several times, working out as many different shapes as possible. When you get three or four that you really like, try out some of the methods you discovered while experimenting with texture earlier and see how they can be related to your pots. Just remember to keep your decoration to the scale of the pot. If you are making a vase which will hold fresh flowers, you will at least have to glaze the inside of the pot. Follow the instructions on pages 84–5. These pages will also tell you how to glaze the outside of the vase. As in all projects in this book, however, the emphasis is on forming methods and decoration with texture; the glaze treatments should be as straightforward as possible. After glazing, the vase is ready to be fired. If you have made a number of pinch pots, you can at this point take them to your local kiln. Do not arrive with one pot in hand, no matter how proud you might be of your work, for firing a single piece is costly and impractical.

Form a clay ball by slapping and rolling it in your hands. Rotate the ball in one hand while making an opening with the thumb of the other. Pinch the walls of the form to an even thickness all around and to the desired shape. By working slowly and pinching evenly as you work, a maximum of control can be achieved. Your hands should be kept dry while shaping. Avoid using water; it will tend to muddy and weaken the clay

 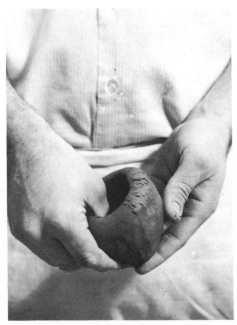 

Completed small pinch pot with incised textured surface
fired at Orton cone 4 with a salt glaze

For a vase with a narrow top, fold the walls over themselves at intervals and continue pinching until walls
are smooth and symmetrical. A light beating with a ruler and smoothing with your fingers will help finish
the form. A lip can be added by bending back the top of the walls. Texture the surface as you wish. A
small stick was used to carve the design here. When the pot is finished, tap the bottom gently on the table
to flatten.

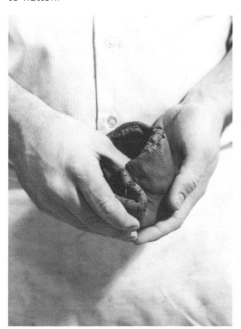 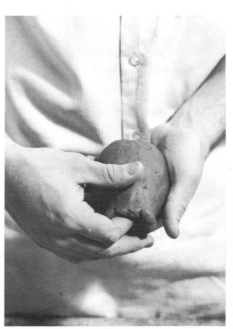 

(Above) Hanging plant pot by John Masson

(Left) Porcelain covered jar by Sema Charles

(Below) Trays made by turning up slab edges.
By Toshiko Takaezu

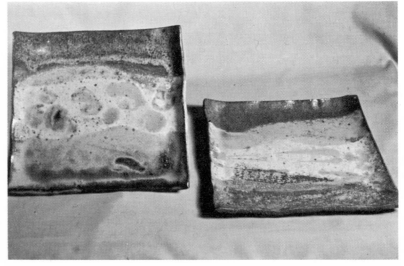

Slab Portfolio

Here are several examples of work done exclusively with slabs to show the versatility of this technique before you start slab projects of your own. A tray can be made effectively by taking a slab and merely turning up the edges, or a simple plant pot by bending a slab into a cylindrical shape and boldly pinching the seam, as was done to make the pots in the photograph bottom right. The hanging plant pot, left, was made by pressing the centre of a slab into a shallow mould, then when the clay hardened, holes were cut for the cords from which it hangs. The piece below left was done by joining seven small slabs. The variations are endless. The main thing to keep in mind is the character of the slab; don't try to make it look like something other than what it is. Also remember that it is ideal for surface effects and can often be enhanced by overall texture – achieved by making the slab on hessian or some other coarse material or surface.

(Top) Plant holders by author. See following page

(Right) Slabs rolled into cylindrical shapes, pinched together, and added to wheel-thrown bases. By John Masson

(Below) Multicoloured pot by Sophia and John Fenton

Plant Holders

A SIMPLE SLAB PROJECT

No matter what part of the country you live in, there are many kinds of fascinating plants or wild flowers which you might like to display, and in this slab project you can make a plant holder which can be hung on the wall. Aside from the weeds or flowers themselves, the interest here will come from the way you treat the surface of the slab, using the techniques set forth in the section on 'Experimenting with Texture' (pages 28–9). Since the holders are quick and easy to make, try doing several, so that you can group them in an arrangement. This same design could also be used to make pencil holders.

Plant holder with hessian impression ready for glazing and firing

Roll out clay on hessian and cut a slab approximately 200 mm × 127 mm (8 in. × 5 in.) and two strips about 25 mm × 127 mm (1 in. × 5 in.) and 13 mm × 64 mm ($\frac{1}{2}$ in. × $2\frac{1}{2}$ in.). Lay the larger strip near the bottom of the slab and the other at top centre so that the two ends are on the slab and the rest hangs over the edge

Join strips to slab base by beating them lightly with a paddle. With a pencil make several indentations in the bottom strip. Punch a hole through the top strip. The slab will hang by this on a nail or hook. Let the holder dry, then glaze and fire

Trivets

A SIMPLE SLAB PROJECT USING PLASTER STAMPS

This is a slab project that is almost foolproof for the beginner. In fact this one, which utilizes the carved plaster stamps made earlier (pages 30–31), would be a welcome gift glazed in colours to match the decoration of a friend's kitchen, breakfast room, or patio. If you have made several plaster stamps, as was suggested, they can be used singly or in combination, and the impressions can be scattered or used as an overall design. A hot plate usually holds a pot or casserole with a flat bottom, so it is a good idea, when you are finished, to beat the tile lightly to insure a level surface.

For two trivets cut one slab – this will be cut in half later. Have slab slightly larger than the sizes you want both trivets to be since it will not hold its shape during stamping and will have to be trimmed afterwards. Press a design with a stamp. Trim outer edges and divide slab in two, then beat. Dry, glaze and fire

Roll out two slabs on a coarse material, such as hessian, and cut to approximately 254 mm × 200 mm (10 in. × 8 in.) and 127 mm × 127 mm (5 in. × 5 in.). Bend the larger slab into a cylinder and join its sides by pressing one into the other with your thumb. Trim one end of cylinder and place it, trimmed end down, on second slab. Cut excess clay from base to align with cylinder

Turn cylinder, with base upside down, and with your fingers join base to the sides. Right the cylinder so that it rests on base and join interior seams, then trim top of pot

Cylindrical Vase

CREATING A CYLINDRICAL FORM USING SLABS

This project gives you the opportunity to use a slab with an overall texture; as described in the section on forming slabs (page 27). Although a cylindrical vase such as this can be any height, the one here is about 178 mm (7 in.) tall, perfect for many short-stemmed flowers. Because of the overall texture and the additional stamping and carving, the rich surface of this pot would look very well in unglazed clay, but the interior would have to be treated since the vase must hold water. In the example shown, the stamping and carving were combined in one area, but you can make other designs; the variations are endless and are limited only by your imagination. NOTE: make the slab at least 13 mm (½ in.) thick so that it will not crack when you bend it into a cylinder.

Completed vase fired at Orton cone 4; the inside is entirely glazed so that the vase can hold water

Retouch textured areas made smooth during handling by pressing a piece of hessian into the clay. Decorate with stamp and carving; or in a different manner if you prefer. When the pot is dry, it is ready for glazing and firing

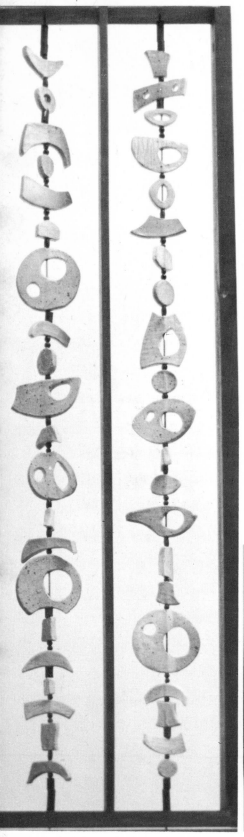

Ideas for the Slab Method

Of all the hand-building techniques, the slab method is the most versatile and offers the most opportunities for creative exploration. Before continuing to other planned slab projects, here are a few illustrations of work done with this technique to help you with ideas of your own. As you can see in photographs on both pages, craftsmen have used the slab method with flair and originality for screens or room dividers. Particular notice should be taken of the wind chime at right with whimsical faces incised in free-form slabs; this could not be done as effectively in any other technique. The unglazed stoneware, is an appropriate example of the versatility of the slab. The crèche from Mexico, at the top of the opposite page, was made by folk artisans who used slabs for the manger, painting them with dark brown slip, then freely modelling the figures inside. The wall mural below right was made of several slabs with applications of other slab forms and freely modelled shapes; the work was then glazed. Since most clay, particularly glazed high-fire ware, is able to withstand the elements, it is possible to make projects for both indoor and outdoor use. Tiles which can be cemented into a kitchen, bath, or patio are still another approach to this process.

(Left) Room divider or screen made with varied shaped tiles and strung vertically in open wood frame panels, size 1·2 m × 2·4 m (4 ft. × 8 ft.). By Henry Lin. Courtesy of Craft Horizons

(Below) Hanging free form planter made with slabs, unglazed, by Robert Winokur. Courtesy of the American Craftsmen's Council

(Above) Sculptured forms shaped from coils combined with slabs to create this Mexican crèche
(Right) Wind chime made by stringing small decorated circular slabs together and hanging from a wooden bar. By Robert and Paula Winokur
(Below) Ceramic wall relief. After piece is developed, it is cut into squares to fit into kiln for firing, then reassembled. Size 610 mm × 965 mm (24 in. × 38 in.). By Henry Lin

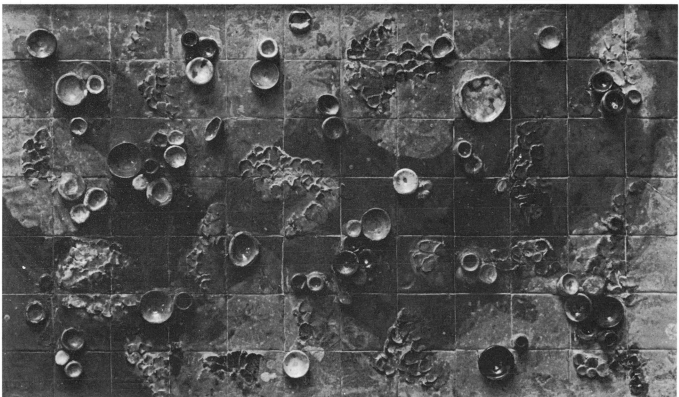

Using the technique described on page 27, with a wire cut six slabs from a rectangle of wedged clay, each about 127 mm × 254 mm (5 in. × 10 in.) and 13 mm ($\frac{1}{2}$ in.) thick. Let slabs set, then score edges that will be joined in making the four sides of pot, scratching them with a pin tool or a fork

Before assembling slabs add soft clay or slip (see glossary) to the scored edges. Join the edges of two slabs and work them together with a modelling tool

Covered Jar

RECTANGULAR SHAPES

The purpose of this project is to give you the experience of making a four-sided piece with handles and cover. An additional point of interest here is the pinching method of sealing the joins. Besides serving to cement the sides, this method adds a decorative quality.

After you have made the slabs necessary for the jar, let the clay dry until it is stiff but still wet enough so that you can pinch it. If you don't allow the slabs to stiffen, they may collapse during construction of the project. This applies to all slab work. Another general rule is to make all joins inside a slab pot as strong as possible by scoring and adding bits of fresh clay. That is, make scratches across the joining areas with your pin-on-stick tool or more practically, a fork. Then add bits of clay to the scored areas and push them into the scratches, smoothing over the seam with your fingers. Since the finishing of a slab pot usually cannot be done until the clay is very stiff (but not leather-hard), you may like to work on more than one piece at a time.

Add the third slab in the same manner. If desired, an ever stronger join can be achieved by laying a coil of clay along the seam and working it in. Add fourth slab. This must be stiffer than the others to support itself during application

Continued on next page

Covered jar – continued from previous page

Turn four sides upright and place on another slab which will be the base. Cut off excess clay and join the base on the inside. You can pinch the outer seams of the pot together to strengthen the construction and to decorate

To make the cover, cut a piece of clay 152 mm (6 in.) square and attach a strip of clay, the same size as the handles, to the centre of it. When this slab is placed on top of the jar, it will adjust to the contour of the neck

Cut a piece of clay about 50 mm × 205 mm (2 in. × 8 in.) and wrap it around the top of the jar to form the neck. Work it in with a fettling knife, again from the inside. Cut two strips of clay for handles and attach these to the sides of the jar, top ends first, using the fettling tool and your fingers to join them to the form

Trim the cover slab so that it is in proportion to the jar. Allow jar to dry thoroughly, then glaze and fire. Do not keep the cover on the pot while drying or firing

Cut three slabs, each approximately 152 mm × 314 mm (6 in. × 12 in.), for the sides of the lantern. Score the upper sides along the 305 mm (12 in.) edges, then spread slip on all scored areas. Put one slab flat and attach the scored edge of another slab to it and work edges together with a fettling tool on the inside where they join. Smooth the outside join with your finger so that it will be strong enough to hold the slabs at a right angle. Join the remaining slab in the same manner

Bend the upright slabs together to form a triangle, joining the upper seam by pinching the clay. Turn upright and pat all edges until smooth with a ruler or a small piece of wood. Let clay stiffen for a while, then sketch a design on the sides

Garden Lantern

TRIANGULAR SHAPES

This slab-built lantern constructed of three sides was designed for outdoor use, but it would also be effective indoors among an arrangement of house plants or suspended with several other slab lanterns, each of a slightly different size. The lantern is designed to be illuminated either with a small electric light bulb or with a candle, and you should choose which you will use before starting the project. If electrified, the bulb will be at the top, if the lantern is suspended, or at the bottom, if it is self-supporting. Also, while you enjoy seeing a candle through the cut-outs in the sides, it is more aesthetically pleasing if an electric bulb is concealed by lining the inside with rice paper. Although the lantern we will make here is triangular, round or square-sided ones can be made using the same general approach. This is another project that would look well unglazed, but if you decide to give it colour, remember that the cut-out designs are the strongest element.

When the clay is leather hard, cut out the designs. Trim the top of lantern so that it is even and cut a top for it from another slab. Score all edges of the cover and the top of lantern. Lightly beat the cover into place. If the lantern is going to be suspended, you will need a hole for a cord made from a small slab of clay

Smoothed coils with stamp decoration. By S. Elliot Sayles

Open coil construction by Rose Krebs

Coils worked in with modelling tool. By Ellen King

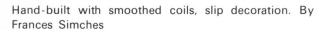

Wheel-thrown pot combined with coils, unglazed. By Karen Karnes

Hand-built with smoothed coils, slip decoration. By Frances Simches

Coil Portfolio

The building of coil upon coil was the way primitive man made his pots, and it was this easy method of gradual building that eventually suggested the wheel. At one period, coil work was done in a production-line manner with one man sitting at a turntable on the ground, rotating it and laying on a rope of coil which another craftsman would make and feed to him over his shoulder. The man at the turntable soon learned that if water and pressure were used when the turntable was rotated, the walls of a pot would rise and become thinner. Potters later discovered from using the turntable that clay could be made to rise without the use of coils. With speed, water, and the proper handling, clay could be thrown and pulled up. Thus, the potter's wheel evolved, and production became much faster. Because of the feeling of structure which you can get with coils, the next few projects will give you work different in feeling from the slab exercises. The coil itself can be allowed to show or it can be smoothed over.

(Right) Large patio bottle with coils partially smoothed. By the author

(Below left) Coil built vase, partially smoothed to achieve ridged effect. By Frances Simches

(Below right) Coil built pot that has coils worked in for scalloped pattern. By S. Elliot Sayles

Pat out a small slab of clay about the size of the palm of your hand. Cut a circle from it, about 76 mm (3 in.) in diameter and 10 mm ($\frac{3}{8}$ in.) thick. Remove the excess clay. Circle this base with a series of coils to form the walls of the pitcher. As you work, join the coils on the inside of the pot with a modelling tool

Direct the coils outwards at the top to make a spout. For the handle take three 305 mm (12 in.) coils, braid them and flatten with a ruler or small stick

Cream Pitcher

SMALL COIL

Your introduction to coil work is a small pitcher which openly displays the technique used. Small coils will be used for this project since they are easier for the beginner to manipulate. The pitcher will only be 152 or 178 mm (6 or 7 in.) high and will be rolled rather than pinched into shape. For one pitcher you will need up to twelve coils, each approximately 305 mm (12 in.) long, but I suggest that you make twice this number and work on two pitchers simultaneously. During coiling, one pitcher may begin to weaken, and you will have to stop and let it stiffen for a while before beginning again. As was illustrated previously, to make coils roll out balls of clay on a slightly damp board, working with both hands from the centre outwards. A damp board is particularly necessary when making small coils since it prevents them from drying out and breaking. Cover the finished coils with a damp cloth. The pitcher will have to be glazed on the inside, whether you are going to use it at the table or as a small vase. The outside need not.

Attach the handle directly behind the spout by smoothing the clay to the coiled body of the pitcher. The pot is now ready to be dried, glazed, and fired

Roll out a lump of clay into a circular shape, about 305 mm (12 in.) in diameter. Cut into an even circle. As you work along, squeeze out large, snake-like ropes of clay about 25 mm (1 in.) thick. Build the bottle by winding these clay ropes around the circular base

After each coil is added, pinch it securely to the previous one. Score all coils on the inside to make a good join all around. If you find it necessary to interrupt your work, be sure to deeply score the top of the pot before you begin again

Patio Bottle

LARGE COIL

Coils can be used on a wheel-built pot to increase its size – a pot is thrown to its maximum height, large coils are joined on and built up to make the pot larger – but exclusive use of coils is the best way of making the bottle of this project. This is by far the largest work presented in this book, and from my teaching experience one of the most exciting as it gives the beginner a chance to make something of size and scope. However, since the piece is about three feet tall, make sure that you have a large enough kiln available to fire it. If you don't have a kiln large enough, adapt the project to the size that is available to you. If you like, you can take several days to finish the bottle, covering the top with a sheet of plastic each time you stop. The base will then be able to dry out while the upper part remains damp and workable.

When the desired height is reached, cut a slab strip large enough for two handles, about 64 mm (2½ in.) wide, 203 mm (8 in.) long, and 13 mm (½ in.) thick, and shape to bottle. Add rim of 25 mm (1 in.) thick clay and smooth by patting with a stick. Since this is a large piece, it will take longer to dry before being glazed and fired

Cut a 127 mm (5 in.) circle from a slab of clay and make two holes in its centre; this will be for the light bulb cord or any other support. Roll out at least a dozen small coils, about 305 mm (12 in.) long, and cover them with a damp cloth. Circle three rows of coils around the slab, scoring them to the base on the inside for a firm join

With the other coils, build up the form until it is about 205 mm (8 in.) high. Experiment and arrange coils to your own design. Score the coils on the inside where they touch. Let the clay stiffen for a while, then turn the piece upside down

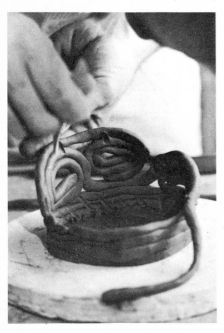  

Hanging Lamp

FREE FORM COILS

In the first two coil projects, the construction was relatively pre-planned – that is, you built up coils in circles until a form was completed. This hanging lamp, on the other hand, gives you freedom to use your ingenuity. As you can see from the photographs, coils are snaked around, back and forth on top of themselves, rather than round and round, to build the lamp. This is a project I have given my classes at Art School, and the students have usually had more fun with it than any other. Whatever you do, don't try to follow exactly the example shown. Do whatever your imagination dictates. If you don't like what is happening, wad the clay up and begin again. This is one of the great virtues of clay: it is cheap, and you don't have to be overly cautious with it. As to finishing the lamp, an all-over glaze in one of the many earth colours could work very well, particularly since you might want to hang it in a corner of your garden. If used indoors, the convoluted shapes of the coils make intriguing patterns on the walls around it.

Add more coils to the top, allowing them to stand about 76 mm (3 in.) high. This is the way the lamp will hang after it has dried, been glazed, and fired

Select a bowl whose shape you like, coat the inside with vaseline or cooking oil, and pour in enough plaster to duplicate form. (See pages 30–31 for directions on mixing plaster.) Let the plaster harden, then separate from the bowl

A Simple Bowl

PRESS MOULD

One of the most direct ways of duplicating a shape is by the press mould method. The bowl shown here or a series of bowls which are made with this technique can be either glazed or unglazed; however, here is a good opportunity to try your hand at some simple brushwork (see pages 88–9). This bowl can also serve as the point of departure for future pots, acting as a base to which coils or slabs can be added. By adding a coil-built stem, it could easily become a compote. Although the instructions are for a plaster mould, one of clay could work just as well.

NOTE: whenever using a clay mould, place a piece of hessian or cloth on it before laying on the slab of fresh clay, or the two will stick together.

With mould inverted, press a clay slab onto it. Cut away the excess and smooth. Make a ring with a coil of clay for the foot of the bowl. Beat the foot until you have an even surface, then score. (Leave the bowl on the mould for about twenty minutes so that it hardens some but does not dry completely, for clay shrinks when drying, and the pressure from the plaster will make it crack.) Remove from mould, dry completely, then glaze and fire

Press Mould Hot Plate

A press mould can be made in two ways: a shape can be hollowed out from a plaster slab by carving, or a form can be built up with clay, then covered with a layer of poured plaster. Once the plaster has set, the clay is removed. Remember that in either method you are making a negative pattern, and that the depressions you carve will be projections in the positive pattern. A simple geometric design is recommended for the beginner.

Take handfuls of clay and press them firmly into the mould. Make a bottom layer so that you can feel the clay going into the depressions of the mould. Then fill in with more clay until the level is slightly higher than the surface of the mould. With a ruler or stick, level the clay so that it is even with the top of the mould. Let the clay harden for a short time, then lift it gently from the plaster. Allow to dry, then glaze and fire

A slip casting mould is made of plaster and comes in two parts which lock together. It has a cavity for the slip to collect and harden. Place the two halves of the mould together and pour slip into the channels leading to the inside space. Allow slip to set for at least fifteen minutes

Remove the top half of mould, exposing the plate. With a fettling knife trim off the extra clay where the slip was poured through the channels

Dinner Plates

SLIP CASTING

If you feel you would like to make a set of dinner plates, you would find it a difficult task with only slab and coil techniques at your disposal. I suggest that for this purpose you look into the many slip casting moulds that are available through the suppliers on page 95, and then buy the one which makes a shape that pleases you most. You can decorate each of the plates individually if you wish. However, limit the decoration on them to glazing as any texturing other than a light stroke around the outer edge will only catch food as well as make cutting on the plate impossible. Since you will be using slip for these plates, you can finish the plates with any of the various stoneware glazes. Striking abstract designs can be done by brushing, pouring, and even splattering glazes of two or three colours. It doesn't matter if they make a pool in the centre. When the plates come out of the kiln, the glazes will have fused to form a smooth, glossy surface, and the depth of colour will be really impressive.

Lift the finished plate from the mould and texture it in any manner you choose. The edges of this plate were not smoothed in order to retain a handmade look. Let dry thoroughly before glazing and firing. Although this method insures uniformity in duplication, subtle differences can occur which will add individuality and interest to the total set

To make three cups, begin with a plaster cup mould and three slabs of clay about 13 mm ($\frac{1}{2}$ in.) thick, cut slightly wider than the mould is high. Wrap one of the slabs around the mould, pressing it together at the seam and then all over to make an even shell

Trim off the excess clay at the top. Remove the mould and let the clay harden for at least fifteen minutes. Repeat process for each mug

Set of Mugs

PRESS MOULD

In this variation of the press mould, a set of mugs is quickly made by wrapping slabs of clay around a cylindrical form. The form is again a plaster mould, this time made by pouring plaster of Paris into a paper cup (of the size desired) and, letting it harden. (Refer to the directions for mixing plaster of Paris in the section on plaster stamps, pages 30–31.) Once the cup has been made, take some care in smoothing the inside so that it can be washed easily. The outsides can be finished with glaze and/or texture. Since you are making a set, invent a theme for the decoration even though each piece will be a variation. This is one of the most practical projects in this book and one which you may return to often. As was suggested with the slab trivets, a set of these mugs would make an excellent gift.

Cut strips for handles about 25 mm × 102 mm (1 in. × 4 in.), or slightly larger than desired. (Clay will shrink during drying and firing.) Add handle to cup by pressing ends, top first, then proceed with decoration. In mugs shown above a scored coil was wrapped around the upper part of each

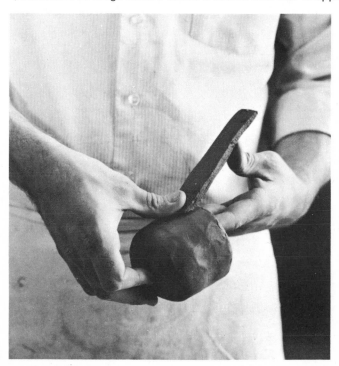

Build up a form with wet sand and texture the surface with a blunt tool. Keep the sand damp so that the form will not crumble. Dig the sand away from the base and carefully pour a thin layer of plaster over the form. If you are working on the beach, remember that FRESH WATER must be used to make the plaster. When this plaster has set a bit, pour on another thin layer. Repeat until shell is about 76 mm (3 in.) thick. When hard, remove and allow to dry for about a week. If the model remains on the beach, cover at night with a sheet of plastic

When the plaster is completely dry, line the inside with a slab of clay, pressing it onto the irregular surface. Patch areas with additional clay where necessary. Completed shell should be about 13 mm (½ in.) thick

Plant Pot

SAND CASTING

The mould technique that is presented here is probably the most fun, since it uses sand and gives you a chance to work outdoors. If you live near the sea, beach sand is ideal. If you don't, the kind you buy at a hardware store will do just as well. The technique we are using is called sand casting, and the result is a fairly large, strongly textured plant pot. Not only does this process allow you to repeat the object, but it gives you a large-size pot with an entirely different quality than that of coiling or slab-building. You begin by modelling one half of a pot form about 305 mm to 457 mm (12 in. to 18 in.) long in wet sand. This design is then coated with plaster, which forms the mould. After the mould has hardened, two clay shells are made in it, for the two halves, which are then joined to make the body of the pot. The process could also be used to make one-piece castings, such as bird baths, and platters.

Grains of sand lining the shell will create texture. When the clay has dried in the mould for about twenty minutes, remove and let stiffen. Repeat process. Join the two halves by scoring their edges and adding slip before pressing together. Hold for a few minutes until the slip starts to dry. Add a thick coil of clay for a base. Cut a

hole in the top of the bottle and add a thick coil of clay for a neck, pressing it firmly to the body of the bottle. Dry, then glaze and fire

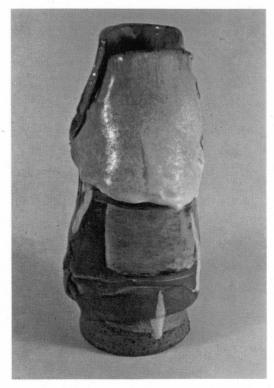

(Above) Vase built up with slabs on a wheel-thrown base. By Len Stack

(Right) Slab cylindrical bottles with thrown tops and bases by John Masson

(Below) Thrown and slab covered jar by Bob Arneson

Combined Methods Portfolio

Once you have learned the basic techniques of hand-built pottery, you can expand the possibilities of these methods by combining or using them together – coil with slab, slab with mould, coil with mould, or coil with slab and mould. The play of one type of construction against another gives exciting contrasts of form and surface which are not available with one technique alone; later on, when you have learned how to throw on the wheel, you will find the combination of thrown and hand-built methods particularly exciting. The pots at the right, for example, were made by throwing cylindrical forms, then wrapping slabs around them, and beating them onto the thrown shapes. The pots at the left were constructed by bending and pinching slabs into tall cylinder shapes, then adding wheel-thrown necks and bases. The next projects will show you ways to combine the approaches demonstrated thus far. While working, think of some other pots that you could make with slab, coil, and mould methods. When you have a good idea, make a note of it or sketch it for future use. The examples on these pages only hint at the possibilities.

(Top right) Flasks by Dennis Parks and *(below)* bottle and vase by Winifred M. Holt

Prepare a slab of wedged clay, about 254 mm × 127 mm (10 in. × 5 in.), several small coils, and a plaster stamp. You will also need the pin tool. Stamp a design on the slab. Trim the long sides so that the slab curves in, or leave it as a rectangle. With your hand under the centre, lift the slab so that it falls into an arc

Take one of the coils and circle it into a cylinder just wider than the base of a candle. Remember that clay shrinks when it dries. Attach cylinder to the slab by scoring its base. Smooth the join, or leave the score marks as is for a decorative effect. Prepare two short coil cylinders for the sides. Cut at an angle to fit the slope of the slab base. Then attach

Candle Holder

SLAB, COIL, WITH PLASTER STAMP

Two basic techniques and a decorative device–slab, coil, and the plaster stamp – are combined to make an arc-shaped candle holder. This is another project which lends itself to many variations, and feel free to make your own adaptations. As you begin to master many of the basic principles of pottery you no doubt will have more confidence in your abilities to work out original designs. A series of candle holders following the basic plan could be made, with different stamps used on each as well as different placement of the coil holders. And the base slab does not have to curve in. It could remain a rectangle or take the form of a gentle S-shape. Since this is not a time-consuming project, play around with it before deciding on a piece, or pieces, to be glazed and fired. Don't labour too hard on any one; the more spontaneous the approach, the better the result.

Make another coil cylinder for the top and attach. The piece when dry is ready to be glazed and fired

Prepare two slabs, each 204 mm × 318 mm (8 in. × 12½ in.), one slab 102 mm × 204 mm (4 in. × 8 in.) and roll out six coils at least 305 mm (12 in.) long. Have ready on your work table a plaster stamp, a ruler or beater, a fettling knife, and a pin tool. With the stamp, make a row of impressions down the centre of one of the larger slabs. From the smaller slab cut a circle about 102 mm (4 in.) in diameter for the base of the vase. Cut a 76 mm (3 in.) strip lengthwise from the other large slab and wrap it round the base. Score inside and pinch on the outside to secure firmly. With the coils, build up the wall of the pot, circling them around two or three times. Score the coils on the inside to each other and to the slab

Trim the stamped slab, leaving narrow margins on either side of the impressed design, and add it onto the coils, again joining on the inside. Take the leftover 25 mm (1 in.) strip and set it onto the inside rim of the stamped slab, so that the entire thickness of the stamped slab protrudes. Join and score

Small Vase

SLAB, COIL, WITH PLASTER STAMP

This vase, an example of the combined method technique, is a cylindrical form, partially glazed, with handles, using the slab, coil and plaster stamp. I suggest that you go through the project once as is and then work out your own version. Unless you are using a high-fire stoneware body, if the vase is to hold water at least the inside will have to be glazed. Some glaze on the exterior might be effective, but I advise caution for the construction is the pot's own decoration.

From the remaining clay, cut two strips 102 mm × 25 mm (4 in. × 1 in.), for the handles and apply them to the form, upper ends first. Smooth the vase to the point of refinement you want, but don't overwork. Dry, glaze, and fire

Prepare five slabs each about 152 mm × 254 mm (6 in. × 10 in.) and 6 mm to 13 mm ($\frac{1}{4}$ in. to $\frac{1}{2}$ in.) thick. Also have a simple bowl-shape mould (see page 56) for the base and press one of the slabs over it

Trim the excess clay and add foot rim, as on page 56. Let stiffen for about twenty minutes, then remove it from the mould

Teapot

SLAB AND PRESS MOULD

Mould and slab techniques are used to make a teapot which is functional and decorative. There are several things to keep in mind here. If you want to brew loose tea leaves in the pot, do not cut a hole for the spout as directed, but instead make a series of small holes. You must be careful, however, that they do not later become plugged with glaze. The position of the spout is also important. Its point must be at a level near the top of the pot, and its base should not be too low, or the teapot will hold very little liquid. The thinner you make your slabs for this project the better, as you do not want the pot to be too heavy when filled. If possible, make this project with a stoneware body. But no matter what clay you use, be sure the teapot is at room temperature or has been slightly warmed before pouring boiling water into it.

To build the sides, cut a 127 mm (5 in.) strip from one of the slabs, long enough to fit around the form. Cut a second strip of clay 102 mm (4 in.) wide and place it just within the diameter of the first. Place it on top; join and score all seams

Continued on next page

Teapot – continued from previous page

Join by scoring and smoothing the clay on the inside and working the two sections together on the outside with your finger. From one of the slabs make a cylinder which will be the spout of the teapot

Cut two strips of clay about 76 mm × 13 mm (3 in. × ½ in.) for the lugs. The bamboo handle will be attached to these after firing. Join them to the teapot, upper ends first

Place the spout on the side of the pot, and, with a pencil, mark where it will join. Within this area make either several holes, or one hole which will correspond with the inside diameter of the spout. Join spout to teapot and smooth seam

For the cover, cut a 127 mm × 127 mm (5 in. × 5 in.) slab and a strip of clay the same size as the lugs. Shape handle to the top of the slab. Place the cover on top of the pot and bend the corners down so that it fits comfortably. If it is too large, trim to fit. After teapot is thoroughly dry, glaze and fire, then attach bamboo handle to lugs. Remember to remove cover during drying and firing

Egyptian Paste Jewellery

This interesting and intriguing process was handed down from ancient times. It is necessary here to use Egyptian paste that is commercially purchased or that is made from the recipe given.

The name Egyptian paste comes from a combination of clay and glaze that the ancients used for their distinctive ceramic beads. Modern potters have not, to my knowledge, been able to duplicate the Egyptian recipe, but we have come up with something quite similar. Although it feels like and can be worked the same as ordinary clay – rolled in balls, pinched into squares, patted into slabs and cut – it eliminates half the steps since glaze is already part of the clay body.

There are two recipes for Egyptian paste. One fires with a dry matt finish, and the beads can be fired together in a bowl without sticking. Both recipes, however, only require one firing to arrive at the finished result. The second recipe gives a jewellery that has a glossy, glaze-like finish. Beads made with this recipe must be strung on nichrome wire rather than placed inside pots when fired.

Below are recipes for both versions, as well as the various colourants which can be added. The ingredients can be purchased from the ceramic suppliers listed on page 95. You need only mix them with water until you have a clay-like substance.

Rolling paste into coils

Coils cut into small pieces and shaped, with a hole 3 mm ($\frac{1}{8}$ in.) diameter, bored in each, for stringing

Paste beads ready for firing

EGYPTIAN PASTE RECIPES – ORTON CONE 06–04

Dry – Beads will not stick together when fired

MATT BASE

Silica	75 grams
Copper carbonate	2
Sodium bicarbonate	2
Bentonite	8
Frit, lead	20

Shiny – Beads must be strung on nichrome wire when fired:

GLOSS BASE

Oxford spar	800 grams
Flint	400
China clay	500
Ball clay	100
Sodium bicarbonate	120
Soda ash	120
Whiting	100
Fine white sand	160

COLOURANTS – FOR BOTH RECIPES

Green	3% Chrome
Turquoise	3% Black copper oxide
Blue	1%–3% Cobalt carbonate
Black	3% Manganese dioxide
Brown	3% Red iron oxide

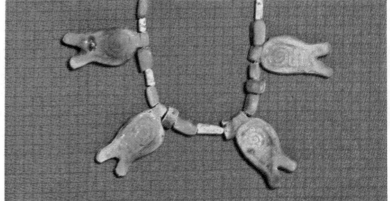

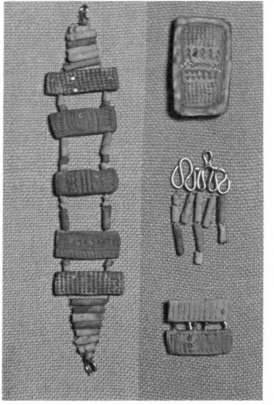

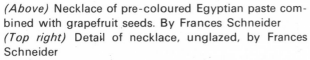

(Above) Necklace of pre-coloured Egyptian paste combined with grapefruit seeds. By Frances Schneider
(Top right) Detail of necklace, unglazed, by Frances Schneider
(Middle right) Detail of necklace, pre-coloured Egyptian paste with incised designs. By Susan Mauss
(Right) Bracelet, pins, and earrings by Susan Mauss

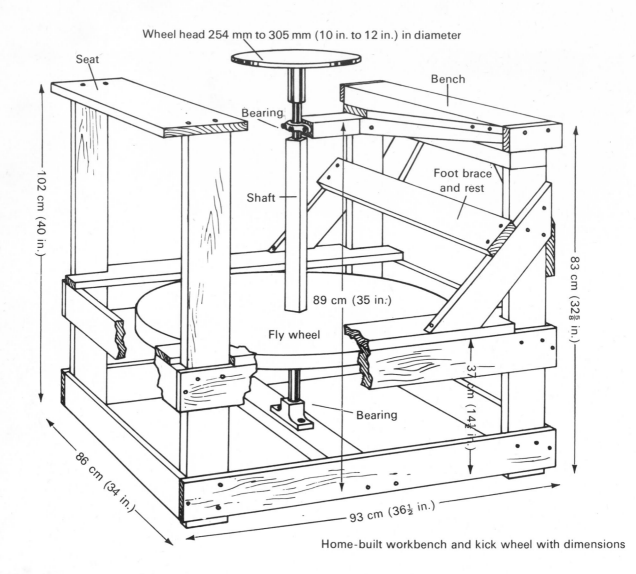

Wheel head 254 mm to 305 mm (10 in. to 12 in.) in diameter

Seat

Bench

Bearing

Foot brace
and rest

Shaft

102 cm (40 in.)

83 cm (32⅝ in.)

89 cm (35 in.)

Fly wheel

37 cm (14½ in.)

Bearing

86 cm (34 in.)

93 cm (36½ in.)

Home-built workbench and kick wheel with dimensions

The Potter's Wheel

If you have a way with a hammer and saw, you can save more than half on costs by building your own kick wheel frame.

The dimensions, such as the height of the bench or the distance between table and bench, can be varied to assure your comfort at the wheel.

For the wheel assembly, you can purchase from certain ceramic supply companies a kit containing the wheel assembly. Components of the kick wheel consist of a 305 mm (12 in.) diameter throwing head, usually marked with concentric circles, and a steel shaft with bearing movement which connects the

throwing head with the balance wheel, weighing approximately 43 kilograms (100 pounds).

Coordinated foot movements on the wheel control starting, speeds in the throwing, and stopping.

Since the method of throwing ceramics on the potter's wheel is the major forming process used by the professional, the reader will want to be as familiar with it as possible and with the terminology used. Not only is throwing the most popular approach to pottery, but it is also the most difficult to master. As stated in the introduction to forming methods, this is an aspect of the medium that you should learn with an instructor. The going may be tough at first, but there is nothing quite comparable to the thrill of seeing clay grow quickly from a hunk thrown on the centre of the potter's wheel to a full, voluminous form.

References to the potter's wheel are found in the earliest hieroglyphic records of the ancient Egyptians, and although there are many types today, none differ much from the first one made 6000 years ago. Potters in the Far East and Middle East use models which are sunk into the ground, and the craftsman squats over it as he throws. Western ceramists use models made so that one sits or stands while throwing. In this country we have both kick wheels and electric wheels. The kick wheel is the direct descendant of the one used by primitive man and is the more popular of the two since control over speed is easily maintained by the foot while the hands are kept on the work.

There are also some good electric wheels on the market, but with them the potter does not have as much control over his work. Although the kind you eventually use will be a matter of personal preference, I believe that one should learn to throw on a kick wheel. On the opposite page, are plans for a simple model which you can build and use at home.

A cylindrical form. This is the basic shape for all wheel-thrown pieces

Cross section of a cylindrical form showing the different stages of development as it is being built on the wheel

Porcelain plates by Sema Charles

Stoneware bottle, partially glazed, by Ellen King

Bottles textured by slip trailing. By John Glick

OPPOSITE PAGE

(Top right) Combination of two pieces, cylinder and base, thrown separately and joined after stiffening. Vase by Bob Arneson

(Bottom left) Bottle, flattened after it was thrown to achieve oval shape, by Len Stack

(Bottom right) Bowl with brushed decoration by Ralph Bacerra

Wheel Portfolio

The examples of ceramics shown here were done on the potter's wheel, and on the following pages are step-by-step photographs that take you through the action of throwing a cylindrical pot. One of the main differences from slab and coil work offered by the wheel is absolute *symmetry* – although a pot can be given a lop-sided effect or be distorted in a number of ways once it has been taken from the wheel (page 83). The clay must be centred, and as the wheel makes several revolutions per second the slightest manipulation with your hands makes an identical change over the entire circumference. Volume is also a consideration in wheel-thrown pots and thrown shapes are as interesting for their outer appearance as for the space they contain. This interplay of inner and outer form is also more peculiar to wheel pots than to those done with slab and coil.

To demonstrate the process of wheel throwing, on the following pages the cylinder is used as the basis for all thrown shapes whether a bottle, a plate, or a bowl. A cylinder can, of course, take a range of forms – low and wide as for a bowl, or tall and narrow as for the bottle shape presented here.

Wheel Throwing

Clay should be perfectly wedged so that it has no bubbles or lumps, and it must be neither too hard nor too soft. Place a ball of prepared clay directly on the wheel or on a moistened bat which is centred on the wheel. Set the wheel in motion and with pressure from the hands work the clay ball to the exact centre of the wheel

Whenever possible join the hands for better control over the clay. Since cylinders tend to flare out, they must be closed in often by 'necking' — a technique that causes walls to thicken and rise

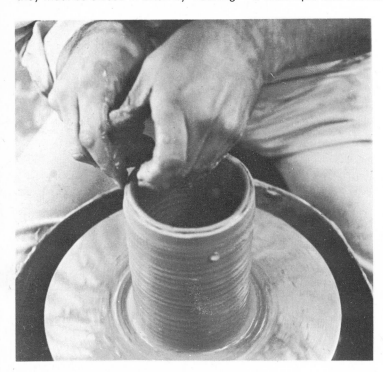

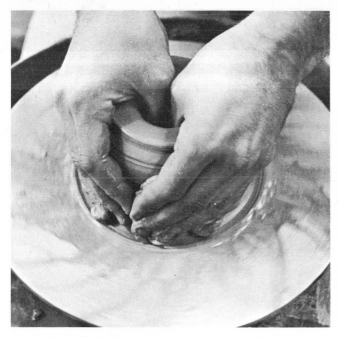

Once the ball of clay has been centred perfectly, open it out with your thumbs. With very little pressure pull the clay up so that it rises into a cylinder

More upward pressure will give a larger cylinder with thinner walls. The uneven top can be cut off with a pin tool

(Top) A wooden modelling tool or pencil is used to trim the excess clay from the base of the finished cylinder

(Centre) To remove the pot from the wheel, hold a wire taut and push it under the base through to yourself. If the pot was thrown on a bat, unfasten the bat from the centre of the wheel and remove with the pot. In this way, the work will not have to be handled until dry

(Bottom) After the pot has been removed from the wheel with a wire, slide it gently off onto a board or plaster bat and allow to dry

Variations

WHEEL-THROWN FORMS

The classical shape of a perfectly symmetrical pot thrown on the wheel is only one aspect of the modern potter's achievement. Often the modern potter uses this as the take-off point for a variety of exciting shapes and forms which reflect his personal approach to the medium. The variations of thrown forms shown on this page are examples. A number of thrown shapes can be combined to make one large work, or the symmetry of a thrown bottle can be deliberately distorted by beating it after it has been removed from the wheel. Forms can be torn and rearranged. Slabs can be added, holes cut, coils circled around. The possibilities are literally endless. The results are rewarding, reflecting as they do the restless search for new, dynamic forms.

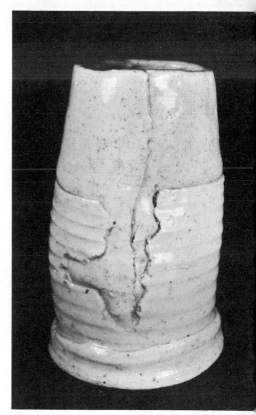

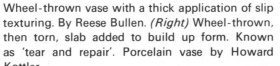

Wheel-thrown vase with a thick application of slip texturing. By Reese Bullen. *(Right)* Wheel-thrown, then torn, slab added to build up form. Known as 'tear and repair'. Porcelain vase by Howard Kottler

(Above) Combined wheel-thrown base clustered onto a thrown base. Stoneware, slip glazed on top section, 508 mm (20 in.) high. By George Kokis

(Right) Wheel-thrown bottle reshaped by forming convex and concave areas with incise texturing. By Robert Winokur

Dipping

Pouring

Pot by Sophia and John Fenton

Bowl by author

Glazing Pots

Following are the four most common methods of applying glaze. Keep in mind that the bottom of a piece is left unglazed, so that it will not stick to the kiln shelf during firing. Either clean off bottom or paint with melted wax before glazing the piece.

Dipping is probably the simplest method, but it requires a large amount of glaze since the bowl or basin used must be full. To glaze a pot one colour, hold it at an angle and dip it into the glaze, turning it quickly and holding it so that as much of the pot as possible is covered. Do not let the layer of glaze become too thick. Touch up unglazed areas with a brush. When glaze is desired only on the outside of a pot, hold the pot by the base and dip straight up and down. The air trapped inside will prevent the glaze from entering.

Pouring is done when a pot is too large to dip or the amount of glaze available is too little. To coat the inside of a pot, pour glaze in until the pot is one-third filled. Twirl the pot around and pour out the excess. Do this quickly since the correct thickness of freshly applied glaze is that of a playing card. Any more may crack or lump. For the outside, lay the pot on two sticks placed over a basin. Pour glaze evenly over and around the pot.

Spraying

Brushing

Bottle by Hui Ka Kwong

Bowl by Ralph Bacerra

Spraying gives an even coating to the pot and more control over thickness but it often wastes large amounts of glaze. It is recommended chiefly for large pots with deep surface depressions and for applying transparent glazes or coloured glaze designs. At times it is hard to tell how thick the glaze is, and the best way to check is by scratching it with a pin. The playing card rule applies also to sprayed glazes.

NOTE: as many glaze materials are toxic, spraying should be done in a booth with an exhaust fan or out of doors.

Brushing is generally used for decorative panels, bands of glaze, etc, but can also be employed for covering an entire pot. Use a wide brush with soft bristles and flow on several coats of glaze for an even application. Apply each coat in a different direction. It is advisable to glaze the inside of a pot first. You can then turn it upside down and work on the outside without disturbing the interior. Oxides or other colourants for decorative designs are best applied with a brush, over the initial glaze if one is used. It helps to have a turntable so that a pot can be rotated while glaze, oxides, and other colourants are being applied.

Firing a Kiln

When loading the kiln be sure the glazed pieces are not touching. Always give the kiln a preliminary heating with the door open to allow the physically combined water to escape from the clay. Heating time should be at least two hours for raw ware, and more for large or especially heavy pieces.

Let the temperature in the kiln rise gradually and uniformly, for if the pots are heated too quickly, they will explode; let the cooling-off time be at least double the firing time. Never open the door of a kiln until the temperature is down to at least 200°C and never open it completely or attempt to unload a kiln until it has dropped to at least 150°C. Firing to low earthenware temperatures should take eight hours; stoneware needs up to ten.

Before purchasing a small electric kiln, check its voltage to be sure your house wiring circuits are adequate to handle it. Take the same safety precautions in firing a kiln as you would when using any other high voltage appliance.

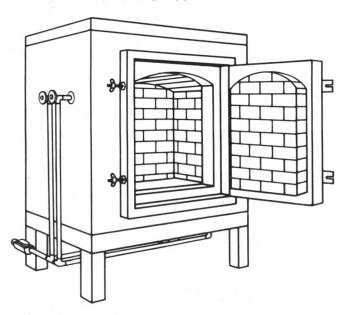

When buying a kiln, be sure the manufacturer is reliable and is equipped to supply replacement parts

Cones

Cones are a temperature indicator that at a predetermined temperature will melt or bend. Usually these are placed at a slight angle in a piece of clay called a cone pat and put in the kiln in such a position as to be visible through the spyhole when the kiln begins to glow. Use a match or a flashlight to check that the cones are lined up with the spyhole. As soon as the desired kiln temperature is reached the cones will melt and fall over, a signal for the kiln to be turned off.

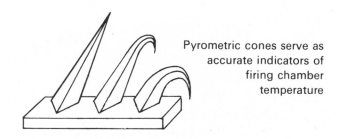

Pyrometric cones serve as accurate indicators of firing chamber temperature

ORTON CONE TEMPERATURE CHART

based on a temperature rise of 150°C per hour

Cone number	Degree centigrade	Cone number	Degree centigrade
H 018	710	H 1	1100
H 017	730	H 2	1120
H 016	750	H 3	1140
H 015	790	H 4	1160
H 014	815	H 5	1180
H 010	900	H 6	1200
H 09	920	H 7	1230
H 08	940	H 8	1250
H 07	960	H 8A	1260
H 06	980	H 8B	1270
H 05	1000	H 9	1280
H 04	1020	H 10	1300
H 03	1040	H 11	1320
H 02	1060	H 12	1350
H 01	1080		

Orton cones are available in two sizes:
P5681 **Large (Standard) cones** approximately 63 mm (2½ in.) high
P5682 **Small cones** approximately 29 mm (1⅛ in.) high

PROGRESSIVE FIRING STAGES

Shrinking	500°C
Physically combined water removed	
Dehydration	500°C–700°C
Clay changes to pottery	
Oxidation	700°C–900°C
Organic matter burned out	

KILN PERIODS FOR FIRING TEMPERATURES

Vitrification	
Red clay	C/04–C/4
Buff clay	C/8–C/10
Bisque firing and floor tiles	C/012
Porcelain	C/10–C/20
Lustres and overglazes	C/022–C/010

STAFFORDSHIRE CONE TEMPERATURE CHART

The collapsing temperature varies to a certain degree upon the kiln firing cycle. A slow firing will cause any particular cone to collapse a little sooner than it would do under a rapid firing schedule and vice versa

Cone number	Degree centigrade	Cone number	Degree centigrade
022	600		
021	614	06	999
020	635	05	1046
019	683	04	1060
018	717	03	1101
017	747	02	1120
016	792	01	1137
015	804	1	1154
014	838	2	1162
013	852	3	1168
012	884	4	1186
011	894	5	1196
010	894	6	1222
09	923	7	1240
08	955	8	1263
07	984	9	1280
		10	1305

Staffordshire cones are available in two sizes:
P5681 **Standard cones** approximately 66 mm (2⅝ in.) high
P5682 **Miniature cones** approximately 25 mm (1 in.) high

It is usual to use a set of three cones: one to bend below the optimum firing point, one at the optimum firing point, and one above. Set them in line so that the angle at which the cones are set allows the cone collapsing first to bend away from the other two.

Open view of kiln.

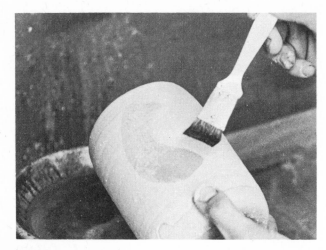

Wax-resist decoration

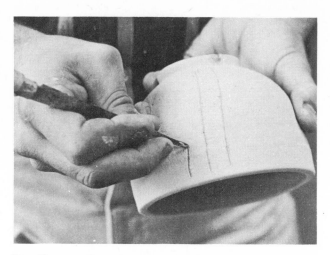

Sgraffito

Tea set by Paul Masson

Detail of bowl by Paul Bellardo

Decorating Techniques

The methods of surface texture described in earlier sections of this book were for clay still in the plastic state. There are, in addition, ways of decorating clay when it is leather-hard, dry, or even after it has been bisque fired.

Wax-resist decoration can be effectively used when clay is in the dry state or after it has been bisque fired. A design is painted on the clay with a solution of thinned wax. When glaze is applied, it will run off the wax areas, giving a design in the clay body colour surrounded by glaze. The wax need not only be applied to the dry or bisqued clay, but also may be brushed onto a layer of glaze with a second coat of glaze sprayed on top. Any wax can be heated over a hot plate and used. Commercial water-soluble wax emulsions are more convenient but give no better results than any paraffin wax.

Sgraffito is a technique also used on both hard and bisque-fired clay. If wax has been applied, a design scratched through the wax with a sgraffito tool gives a sharp linear pattern. More common is to scratch

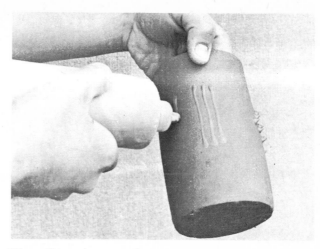

Staining

Slip trailing

Bowl by John Glick

Detail of bottle by Anthony Prieto

a design through the glaze coating of a pot to expose either the body or a preliminary glaze. This is done while the glaze is still slightly damp. If too dry or too thick, it will chip and leave a ragged edge. The object of sgraffito is a sharp, clean line.

Staining is best done when the clay is dry. This is a way of treating clay when you want a burnt, natural looking surface. To make a stain, use two tablespoons of any oxide (such as red iron oxide), the same amount of high or low fire glaze, and half a cup of water. Mix and paint on the area you want stained. Wipe off with a damp sponge. Any impressions in the clay will be darker and the raised surfaces lighter after firing.

Slip trailing is a technique in which slip is trailed over leather-hard clay with a syringe, in much the same way as decorating a cake. The body must not be too dry, however, or the slip will fall off when it dries. A plastic mustard dispenser (shown above) can be as effective as a syringe, and colourants may be added to the slip if desired.

Early Japanese Raku ware bowl. Courtesy of the Brooklyn Museum

Raku

The Raku method of making pottery was developed by the Japanese and named for the great tea master Sen-no-Rikyu. Although Raku means enjoyment, pleasure, contentment, and ease, the actual forming of Raku is far from the pacific connotations of the word, as it is one of the most dramatic and compelling of the modern potter's techniques. A high fire open clay body is used to make a vessel, which is then bisque fired. (The time-consuming bisque process can be shortened by placing the pot freshly made and wet directly in the red-hot kiln to give an instant bisque. Allow no drying to occur, or the pot will explode.) Low-temperature glazes with lead, frit, or borax bases are applied, and the pot is allowed to dry thoroughly. When a kiln has been heated to temperatures somewhere between 800°C and 950°C, the pot is placed in the red-hot oven with long-handled tongs and left inside until the glaze melts, anywhere from a few minutes to an hour, depending on the temperature of the kiln and the glaze used. The process of the ware is checked through the peep hole in the kiln door, and when the pot looks shiny and wet all over, it is removed from the kiln with tongs. Two things can now be done. The pot can be placed directly in cold water, which will cool it instantly, or it can be plunged into a large container of combustible materials such as sawdust, leaves, or wood chips, and then placed in water to cool.

THE RAKU FIRING PROCESS

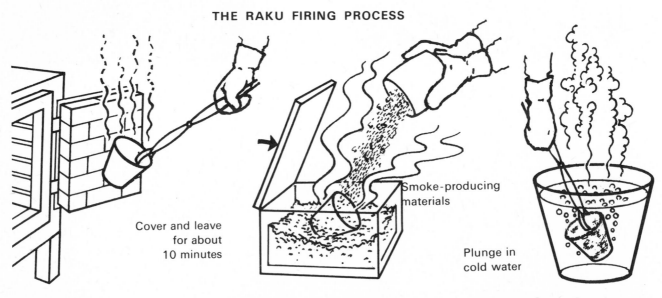

Cover and leave for about 10 minutes

Smoke-producing materials

Plunge in cold water

With long-handled tongs, remove red hot pot from kiln

REDUCTION GLAZE EFFECT FOR SUBTLE NON-REFLECTING COLOURS

OXIDIZING REACTION FOR BRIGHT, SHINY COLOURS

(Above and below) Raku pots, wheel-thrown with engobe decoration. Grey areas developed after firing when pots were exposed to smoke. By Paul Soldner

(Above) Raku bottle, wheel and slab, 254 mm (10 in.) high. The rough texture of the glaze resulted from the Raku firing technique. By the author

Technical Notes

Here are some clay bodies, glazes, and engobes which fire at different temperatures.

Once the base has been weighed, water is added to form a solution – the consistency of milk.

NOTE: If after firing the unglazed clay body is not as dark in colour as you would like, there are two ways to get a darker body: 1) Boil the pot in tea. 2) Use a darkening solution of: 1 teaspoon pyrogollol or pyrogallic acid to 0·568 litres (1 pint) water. Dunk the pot in the solution or paint it on. It will oxidize in the air in a few hours and give a permanent darker shade. Caution: Avoid direct contact with skin.

Earthenware body (Binns)

Ball clay	25
China clay	25
China stone	20
Flint	30

Fire to 1100 °C

Stoneware bodies

Ball clay	8
China clay	8
China stone	8
Quartz	1

Fire from 1250–1300 °C

Ball clay	4
China clay	1
China stone	5

This is slightly translucent if fired to 1250 °C

Porcelain body

China clay	5·5
Feldspar	2·5
Quartz	1·5
Bentonite	0·5

Fire to 1250 °C

Bone china body

Calcined bone	20
China clay	16
China stone	14

Fire to 1200 °C

Orange – Orton cone 04 – 1060 °C

	Weights in Grams
White Lead	83·3
Flint	16·0
Potassium Bicarbonate	6·0
China Clay	8·6
Tin Oxide	5·0

White – Orton cone 04 – 1060 °C

Frit 3304	80
Borax	10
China Clay	5
Colmenite	5

8% Tin Oxide

For Black add:
   3% Red Iron Oxide
   2% Cobalt Oxide
   2% Manganese Dioxide

Opaque White – Orton cone 04 – 1060 °C

Frit 2124	150·0
China Clay	7·5
Zircopax	30·0

Glossy White – Orton cone 9 – 1280 °C

Oxford Feldspar	75·0
Whiting	12·5
Zinc Oxide	5·0

Yellow – Orton cone 4 – 1184 °C

Feldspar 181	900
Flint	600
China Clay	300
Dolomite	300
Colmenite	600

5% Yellow Stain
2% Tin Oxide

Base for Black and Green glazes – Orton cone 4 – 1186 °C

Feldspar 181	120
Kaolin	30
Flint	30
Barium Carbonate	60
Zinc Oxide	30
Colmenite	30

For Black add the following to base:
   20% Barnard Clay
   5% Copper Carbonate
For Green add to base:
   5% Copper Carbonate

Semi-matt – Orton cone 9 – 1280 °C

Eureka Spar	15·0
Volcanic Ash	11·5
China Clay	7·0
Silica	7·0
Whiting	12·7
Tatanium Oxide	6·2

Base, White	Weights in Grams
China Clay	15
Ball Clay	20
Nephine Syenite	30
Flint	20
Borax	5
Zircopax	5
Talc	5

For Black add:
   $\frac{1}{2}$% Black Copper Oxide
   3% Iron Chromate

For Brown add to base:
   3% Red Iron Oxide
   10% Rutile

Glossary

Absorbtion – Soaking up of water by a clay body.

Ball clay – Highly plastic, fine-grained, sedimentary clay, usually added to less plastic clays.

Bat – A plaster slab or disc on which clay is formed or dried. Made by pouring no less than 25 mm (1 in.) of plaster into an oiled pie tin.

Biscuit or Bisque – Unglazed clay fired once at a low temperature (Orton cone 010–04).

Calcine – To heat a ceramic material to a moderate temperature to drive off chemical water and carbon dioxide.

Chemical water – Part of the clay that is driven off by heat, causing the clay to shrink in the firing.

China clay – or Kaolin, one of the components of porcelain, a pure clay that fires clear white.

Clay bodies – Prepared clay. The most common classifications are earthenware, stoneware, and porcelain.

Colourants – Various oxides and carbonates which are able to withstand high temperatures and give colour to glaze or clay body.

Earthenware – A low firing natural clay body usually red or brown when fired to maturity, non-vitreous and porous with comparatively coarse grain structure and low chipping resistance.

Egyptian paste – A self-glazing body that was used by ancient Egyptian potters.

Engobe – A white or coloured thin layer of slip covering a raw or bisque pot, usually to give a harder and smoother surface. It may or may not be glazed over.

Feldspar – Widely found material of several varieties. Orthoclase feldspar, containing potash, is most frequently used in bodies and glazes as an important fluxing agent, and to give a brilliant and waxy appearance to the clay. When decomposed it becomes kaolin.

Flux – Common fluxes are bone ash, frit, feldspar, and lime. They are the lowest melting compound in a glaze.

Frit – A carefully compounded glass which has been fused and fired. Used to render glazes insoluble and make lead non-toxic.

Glaze – Thin coating of special glass, used as a decoration and to seal clay surfaces rendering them waterproof.

Glaze fire – The maturing temperature at which glaze will melt to form a surface coating. Firing ranges vary with the type of glaze.

Grog – Crushed or ground hard-fired clay used to reduce shrinkage or warping and to add texture to the clay.

Incised – Surface designs cut into the clay for decorative purposes.

Kiln – A refractory clay-lined furnace for firing ceramic ware.

Kneading – Wedging or working the clay with fingers to obtain an even texture throughout.

Leather hard – Condition of clay when it is too firm to bend yet soft enough to be carved. Clay in this state can be handled without misshaping it.

Matt glaze – A dull-surfaced glaze, lustreless, and non-reflecting.

Mature – Refers to the development of the desired properties in clays, clay bodies, and glazes.

Overglaze – Decoration of a ware which has already been glazed.

Overglaze colours – Mineral colourants with a lower firing range than the underglazes and not as durable. However the low firing range allows the use of a larger quantity of varied and brilliant colours.

Oxidation – Firing process requiring the presence of oxygen in sufficient quantities to cause combustion of the carbon gases. If not sufficient, some carbon may remain in the ware. A chamber free from smoke and a clear bright flame indicate an oxidized atmosphere.

Plasticity – The property of clay which allows it to be worked and reshaped without cracking.

Porcelain – Hard and non-porous, the most highly refined of all clay bodies and requiring the highest firing. White, and translucent.

Pottery – Term loosely applied to any ceramic form or to the place where it is made.

Pyrometer – An instrument for recording the exact temperature of the kiln.

Pyrometric cones – Slender pyramids of ceramic material made in a graded series. They do not measure temperature; they measure the amount of heat-work done. At certain temperatures they soften and bend indicating to the potter that the clay and glazes which require a certain time and temperature to mature have done so.

Raku – A method of making pottery using a high-fire, porous clay body. Named for the great tea master Seno-no-Rikyu, it was developed by Japanese potters for the tea ceremony.

Reduction – The cutting down of oxygen to produce a smoky atmosphere in the kiln chamber thus allowing carbon to draw oxygen from the clay body and glazes.

Refractory – Material with a high temperature resistance.

Rib – A tool used in throwing a pot and to smooth surfaces.

Salt glaze – Produced by tossing salt into a hot kiln. The salt vapourizes and combines with the surface of the work.

Sgraffito – From the Italian word meaning 'scratched through', done by incising or cutting a design through a coloured slip coating to reveal the clay body or a preliminary glaze underneath.

Shrinkage – Contraction of clay during drying or firing.

Slip – Clay in liquid suspension. Functions as a potter's glue or as decoration.

Slip glaze – A raw glaze made from natural clays.

Slip trailing – Decorative process using an eye-dropper, small rubber syringe, or any substitute to trail slip on clay.

Spray booth – An enclosure used when spraying on glazes. Should be well ventilated to prevent inhalation of harmful glaze dust.

Spy hole – Small observation hole in kiln, wall or door.

Stain – Sometimes a single colouring oxide, but usually a combination of oxides plus alumina, flint, and a fluxing compound. Used in decorating and in colouring glaze.

Stoneware – A hard, vitreous, non-porous, non-translucent body with a wide range of temperature over which it will vitrify. More refined than earthenware and a very useful clay for the potter. Usually buff, tan, or grey when fired.

Throwing – Forming pottery on the wheel.

Translucency – Ability of a clay body to transmit scattered light.

Vitreous – Impurities in the clay which melt upon heating to form glass and act as a bond.

Ware – Pottery in either raw, bisque, or glazed state.

Warping – Distortion in a pot caused by non-uniform drying or uneven ware thickness, or from being fired in a kiln which does not heat evenly.

Wax resist – A method of decoration using warm wax or a wax emulsion applied to either raw or bisque pots or between two layers of glaze. Wax applied to the pot will resist the glaze and will lift off after firing.

Weathering – Rendering the clay more plastic by exposing it to all types of weather.

Wedging – The process of vigorously forcing any air bubbles from the clay in order to obtain a uniform consistency.

Bibliography

Billington, Dora, *The Technique of Pottery*, London, B. T. Batsford Limited, 1962. Fourth impression 1969.

Colbeck, John, *Pottery: The Technique of Throwing*, London, B. T. Batsford Limited, 1969.

Drake, Kenneth, *Simple Pottery*, Studio Vista.

Leach, Bernard, *A Potter's Book*, Hollywood-by-the-Sea, Florida, Transatlantic Arts, Inc, 1956.

Nelson, Glenn C., *Ceramics*, New York, N.Y., Holt, Rinehart & Winston, Inc, 1960.

Wildenhain, Marguerite, *Pottery: Form and Expression*, New York, N.Y., Reinhold Publishing Corp, 1962.

Noble, Joseph V., *The Techniques of Painted Attic Pottery*, New York, N.Y., Watson-Guptill Publications, Inc, 1965.

Rhodes, Daniel, *Clay and Glazes for the Potter*, New York, Greenberg Publishers, 1957.

Nelson, Glenn C., *Ceramic Reference Manual*, Minneapolis, Minnesota, Burgess Publishing Co, 1958.

Marlow, Reginald, ARCA, *Pottery Making and Decorating*, New York, Studio Publications, 1957.

Norton, F. H., *Ceramics, An Illustrated Primer*, New York, Hanover House, 1960.

Green, David, *Pottery Materials and Techniques*, Faber and Faber Limited, 1968.

Green, David, *Understanding Pottery Glazes*, Faber and Faber Limited, 1968.

Röttger, Ernst, *Creative Clay Craft*, London, B. T. Batsford Limited, 1961. Seventh impression 1970.

Schmitt-Menzel, Isolde, *Fun With Clay*, London, B. T. Batsford Limited, 1969.

Sanders, Herbert H., *Pottery & Ceramic Sculpture*, Menlo Park, California, Lane Book Company, 1964.

Eppens, J. H., *Pottery*, New York, Universe Books, 1964.

Suppliers

CLAYS

English China Clay Sales Limited
14 High Cross Street
St Austell
Cornwall

Pike Brothers
Wareham
Dorset

Fulham Pottery Limited
210 New King's Road
London SW6

Potclays Limited
Wharf House
Copeland Street
Hanley
Stoke-on-Trent

Watts, Blake and Bearn Limited
Newton Abbot
Devon

KILNS

Allied Heat Company Limited
Electurn Works
Otherstool Way
Watford By-pass
Watford
Hertfordshire

E. J. Arnold
Butterley Street
Leeds LS10 1AX
Yorkshire

N. Bosson
Cromartie House
Belgrave Road
Longton
Stoke-on-Trent

British Ceramic Services Company Limited
Bricesco House
Wolstanton
Newcastle under Lyme
Staffordshire

Dowson and Mason Gas Plant Company Limited
Alma Works
Levenshulme
Manchester 19

Arthur Homer
Wayside Cottage
St Agnes
Cornwall

Bernard Webber Limited
Phoenix Works
Hanley
Stoke-on-Trent

GENERAL MATERIALS, TOOLS AND EQUIPMENT

E. J. Arnold
Butterley Street
Leeds LS10 1AX
Yorkshire

W. Podmore and Sons Limited
Caledonian Mills
Shelton
Stoke-on-Trent

Wengers Limited
Etruria
Stoke-on-Trent

WHEELS AND OTHER MACHINERY

E. J. Arnold
Butterley Street
Leeds LS10 1AX
Yorkshire

W. Boulton and Company
Burslam
Stoke-on-Trent

Fulham Pottery Limited
210 New King's Road
London SW6

Bernard Webber Limited
Phoenix Works
Hanley
Stoke-on-Trent

TAYLOR ELECTRIC WHEELS AND KICK WHEELS

Fulham Pottery Limited
210 New King's Road
London SW6

BOOKS, TOOLS AND SOME MATERIALS

Alec Tiranti Limited
72 Charlotte Street
London W1

LEACH WHEEL TO ORDER

Woodley's Joinery Works
Newton Poppleford
Devon

Beutlich, Tadek, *The Technique of Woven Tapestry*, Batsford
Collingwood, Peter, *The Techniques of Rug Weaving*, Faber
Kirsch, Dietrich and Jutta Kirsch-Korn, *Make Your
Own Rugs*, Batsford
Rhodes, Mary, *Ideas for Canvas Work*, Batsford
Seagrott, Margaret, *Rug Weaving for Beginners*, Studio Vista
Springall, Diana, *Canvas Embroidery*, Batsford

Also available in this series
**FRAMING, MACRAMÉ, RUGMAKING, JEWELLERY,
WEAVING, CANDLEMAKING, CROCHET**
To be published in 1974
APPLIQUÉ, SOFT TOYS